# Spenser

# Spenser

## Simon Shepherd

*Lecturer in English Drama*
*University of Nottingham*

HUMANITIES PRESS INTERNATIONAL, INC.
Atlantic Highlands, NJ

First published in 1989 by
Humanities Press International, Inc.,
Atlantic Highlands, NJ 07716

©Simon Shepherd, 1989

**Library of Congress Cataloging-in-Publication Data**

Shepherd, Simon.
  Spenser.

  (Harvester new readings)
  Bibliography: p.
  Includes index.
  1. Spenser, Edmund, 1552?–1599—Political and
social views.   2. Marxist criticism.   I. Title.
II. Series.
PR2367.P6S47   1989   821'.3   88–23195
ISBN 0–391–03475–8

Printed in Great Britain

'A great houskeeper is sure of nothinge for
his good cheare, save a great Turd at his gate.
(quoted by Maureen Quilligan, 1983,
from Laurence Stone, 1965,
from a sixteenth-century Gloucester proverb)


Thanks to the usuals are due: to Mick, Maureen and George,
and to Jessica, for helping with the manure.

# Harvester New Readings

This major new series offers a range of important critical introductions to English writers, responsive to new bearings which have recently emerged in literary analysis. Its aim is to make more widely current and available the perspectives of contemporary literary theory, by applying these to a selection of the most widely read and studied English authors.

The range of issues covered varies with each author under survey. The series as a whole resists the adoption of general theoretical principles, in favor of the candid and original application of the critical and theoretical models found most appropriate to the survey of each individual author. The series resists the representation of any single either traditionally or radically dominant discourse, working rather with the complex of issues which emerge from a close and widely informed reading of the author in question in his or her social, political and historical context.

The perspectives offered by these lucid and accessible introductory books should be invaluable to students seeking an understanding of the full range and complexity of the concerns of key canonical writers. The major concerns of each author are critically examined and sympathetically and lucidly reassessed, providing indispensable handbooks to the work of major English authors seen from the new perspectives.

# Contents

# Introduction

The 'reading' which this book proposes is neither very new nor very surprising. An already well-established body of theory is brought to bear on the work of a well-known poet. What could be more logical, more reliable, than the combination of Marx and Spenser?

In the current new critical trend which is overhauling our approaches to the Renaissance, the influence of Marxism can be felt. This trend is called 'New Historicism', and its method is to study a text in its historical context, in relation to social and political events and to other texts. No dividing line is drawn between literary and non-literary texts. All texts may be analysed to produce historical understanding. But New Historicism is a trend rather than a discipline, indeed a bandwagon. There is often little rigour about the selection of other texts which are to provide a context for the text under study. Clearly, different meanings can be made by constructing differing contexts. Furthermore there is a somewhat touristic approach to history, which scrapes surfaces for interesting anecdotes without developing a deep

1

and structured understanding of a historical period. Lack of space prevents me discussing New Historicism properly, but I'd urge you to look at the articles mentioned in the notes to this chapter which are all useful summaries and discussions.

The influence of Marxism can be felt because Marx stressed that people's consciousness of their relationship to the world around them, and that includes the artist's consciousness, is shaped by the concrete needs and pressures of their daily lives. Hence all aspects of a historical context have bearing on the creation of, and our understanding of, a particular text. For the Marxist there is no such thing as a universal text written by a genius who transcends history. If there were such a thing as a universal genius she would have suggested the dictatorship of the proletariat and we wouldn't have been pratting about for five centuries.

But Marxism is played down in certain practices of New Historicism, being replaced by more 'subtle' theories of texts. It is not an unconnected fact that Marxism still retains its status as a political and revolutionary philosophy, and a lot of well-paid academics want to be political enough to be trendy but not political enough to change the world.

My analysis of Spenser is less New Historical than old-fashioned Marxist. I have stressed again and again the importance of class and economics in their influence on Spenser's thought. I am motivated in this partly because the modern trend in general often forgets about class and economics. But specifically Spenser studies have been surrounded for so many years by all sorts of stuff about mythology, iconography, arcane philosophy, neo-platonism and numerology that I wanted to correct the balance and endeavour to show Spenser in a real world, a world in which people have to eat, live, defend themselves, survive.

My motives in doing this are not merely derived from an attempt to make Spenser once again readable for students, rather than being simply the property of scholarly gentlemen's clubs. But also because I take seriously what not only Marxism but some of the very best New Historicism says about the role of the critic. In writing criticism one always writes from a political position (whether one's conscious of it or not). And the critical text always has a political function within educational institutions, which are themselves part of the political structure of the state; criticism can challenge or reproduce dominant ideas (usually it does the latter). My motives in presenting a different reading of Spenser are thus polemical and political—just like everyone else's.

I have tried to keep the overall theoretical approach very simple, always returning to the same point: class and economics. Where I have used more complex approaches I introduce these on the way. Of course there will be people who say that it's all too simple for dealing with the scholarly Spenser (so they think scholars are beyond class analysis!). But also too simple a version of Marxism. I think I have written what is often called vulgar Marxism, because I have not wanted to lose sight of the importance of economics and of real social and material production in a person's life: 'as individuals express their life, so they are. What they are, therefore coincides with their production, both with *what* they produce and with *how* they produce. The nature of individuals thus depends on the material conditions determining their production' (Marx and Engels, *The German Ideology*, p. 42). If I have overestimated the role of the economic, it is by way of compensation for its disappearance from so many other sorts of account. It is important, I think, for us academics, theorists, critics to remember that 'not criticism but revolution is the driving force of history ...' (*The German Ideology*, p. 59).

We do know, by the way, Marx's opinion of Spenser. In his *Ethnological Notebooks* he called him 'Elizabeth's arse-kissing poet' (p. 305). Which seems pretty vulgar. Happy reading!

3

# 1

# Politics

## A. A *View of Ireland*

Spenser was a penpusher in the service of imperialism. Much of his writing was directly concerned with the administration of the English occupation forces in Ireland. But the more closely involved it was, the less we now know about it. Most of his letters and documents remain unpublished; his treatise on Ireland was not printed in his lifetime; but the poems go through constant reprintings, are set for A level exams, and furnish material for career academics. What happens to Spenser may be seen as part of the larger process whereby modern culture has constructed something called 'Literature', which is defined by its artistic merits and floats free of any political and social context; it is also, of course, supposedly produced by those sublime beings, white able-bodied heterosexual men. Our picture of Spenser the writer, the 'sage and serious' Spenser, is built on a suppression of Spenser the penpusher.

This chapter is largely concerned with the politics of Spenser, as expressed both in his own views and in our cultural image of him. It begins with the earliest significant

4

step in the construction of that image. When the state refused to grant a licence for publication of Spenser's *View of Ireland* in 1598 it established the terms on which he was acceptable as a laureate. By starting this chapter with a lengthy analysis of *A View* I intend to give it importance. This is not to say that it is a magical 'key text'. Many of its ideas appear also in the poems, but in *A View*, as the Elizabethan censor realised, they are more unambiguous. There is none of the 'dark conceit' that claims to conceal meanings, none of the esoteric reference which supposedly directs the artwork to an elite audience only. In concentrating its attention on the 'dark conceit' the Spenser industry conceals the brutalities of Spenser's thought and creates around Spenser an atmosphere of elite scholasticism. *A View* has importance to us all now since it grew out of the British suppression of Ireland, the revolting history of which we still live with.

Spenser's *View of the Present State of Ireland* was probably finished in 1596 (though some parts may have been written earlier); it was first published in 1633. It is a description of Ireland, written in dialogue form, which analyses the economy, geography, social structure, history and military occupation in order to make some proposals for an efficient English policy towards this troublesome new colony. The policy ideas had been circulating for some time in the English colonial administration (see Renwick, ed., 1970 for much of this), but it was very much in Spenser's interest to publicise them in England. Spenser's analysis observes three major social groupings that were involved—or wanted to be involved—in the government of Ireland. These comprised the native Irish, the Anglo-Irish feudal families (who were products of an earlier settlement) and the colonial administrators appointed by the Elizabethan government. During Spenser's time in Ireland, relations were tense between the feudal families, who wished to maintain their

5

power, and the new administration, which threatened to limit and override that power. The feudal families derived from the baronial factions who had competed for power on English soil (in those campaigns of aristocratic piracy loosely referred to as the Wars of the Roses). That bloody competition had been ended by the centralised administration of the new Tudor regime; that's to say, it had been ended in *England*. What happened, as is the way with colonies, is that the English exported their violence (in this case, power-hungry inhabitants of the pages of Debrett) to Ireland; and it was in Ireland, while Spenser was there, that the centralised Tudor administration sought to exercise its power against the remnants of a challenging aristocracy. One such contest marked Spenser's earliest years in Ireland, when in 1579 Fitzgerald, Earl of Desmond, allied himself with Spain against England. The rebellion had to be suppressed by the Lord Deputy of Ireland, at this time Arthur, Lord Grey de Wilton, accompanied by his secretary Edmund Spenser. Then, in the late 1590s, at the end of Spenser's career, there was the rebellion of O'Neill, Earl of Tyrone. This rebellion was not so much the disquiet of a baronial family as a fightback by the colonised, native Irish, against the occupying forces. The rebellion failed, but not before it had driven Spenser off his estate in Kilcolman. It was at this time, during these conflicts, that Spenser put together his *View of the Present State of Ireland*.

Before my analysis of A *View* begins, I should explain more fully that I have chosen to start here in order not only to try to clarify some of Spenser's ideas, but also to describe some of the real social context within which Spenser was working. To approach Spenser's ideas from A *View* is to discover a writer who is very hard-headed about the manipulative power of ideology, about the central importance of economics in people's lives and thought, and about the necessity for physical force. It is this aspect of

Spenser's thought which is often underplayed. In turn we can relate this to his class position, and to a widespread ideology of individualism and absolutism, fostered by the Tudor monarchs. The text of A *View* can take us into brief discussion of that royal power and of class relations in England as well as Ireland. Finally, and most radically, it can lead us, as it led Spenser, into a consideration of colony and colonising power which provokes scepticism about the very idea which justifies the process of colonialism, namely English nationalism. So in many ways A *View* takes us into a necessary discussion of social/political context as well as finding a Spenser who is not often presented to us (as I'll show at the end of the section). My method, I should add, is neither to tell a chronological history nor to identify 'themes' in Spenser's writing, but to describe some key elements of a specific context and some key ideas to which they gave rise. These should then be of use in reading works from any part of Spenser's output.

Towards the end of A *View* Spenser demonstrates explicitly what we might have guessed much earlier, that he knows the work of Machiavelli. The Elizabethan state propagandised against Machiavelli, associating his name with evil conspiracy and devils, in order to devalue his ideas. Those ideas drew the hostility of monarchs and churchmen because they suggested that there was nothing either natural or pre-ordained about monarchy, and that the inculcated fear of god was no more than a device for maintaining power by keeping the majority of people in awe. For Machiavelli social relations are power relations, and rule is maintained by force and made respectable and indeed 'natural' by myths, religion, ideology. (The radical potential here is that once you understand a con you can start to dismantle it.) Despite the vilification these ideas, together with those of other European sceptics such as Bodin, Guicciardini, Montaigne, were picked up by English intellectuals.

Spenser could have known about Machiavelli from a variety of sources, perhaps in particular from his early, close friend, Gabriel Harvey. Here are some examples of Machiavellian thought in *A View*: he recommends repairing church buildings 'for the outward show ... doth greatly draw the rude people to the reverencing and frequenting thereof' (p. 223). Religious faith is a device which maintains social order. Spenser complains of the 'base sort' who willingly swear false oaths on the instruction of their lords, concluding 'so inconscionable are these common people and so little feeling have they of God or their own soul's health' (p. 68). Proper respect for god, internalised as care for one's soul, would have the useful effect of breaking these allegiances to enemy lords. Indeed ideological control has perhaps more force than direct terror; 'when a people are inclined to any vice or have no touch of conscience nor sense of their evil-doing, it is bootless to think to restrain them by any penalties or fear of punishment; but either the occasion is to be taken away or a more understanding of the right and shame of the fault is to be imprinted' (pp. 68–69). Ideas of right and wrong are not natural but can be 'imprinted', and thus political control is maintained. Ideas about moral value, as well as ideas about what is natural or proper or possible, may be said to constitute ideology. Spenser is very close to Machiavelli in his stress on the important role of ideology in the state.

A stable society has to be artificially constructed; similarly individual opinion is not instinctive but induced. In line with some theories of rhetoric, human language is seen not as a natural expression of the speaker's mind but, instead, as an influence on that mind: 'the words are the image of the mind. So, as they proceeding from the mind, the mind must be needs affected with the words' (p. 119). Thus the language of conquered peoples, such as the Irish, has to be suppressed. Clothes also function like language: 'the person that is gowned is by his gown put in mind of gravity' (p. 121). The manner or 'condition' of the person does not pre-exist, but results from, the clothing. In these ways, the human individual may be seen to be constructed rather than natural.

The best method of ensuring loyalty is not, however, through ideology but economics. Spenser says a tenant is more prepared to embrace 'change and alteration' if he has no holding, no building on a farm, no costs 'employed in fencing or husbanding the same as might withhold him from any such wilful course as his lord's cause or his own lewd disposition may carry him into'; a tenant can be improved if he is 'drawn to build himself some handsome habitation thereon, to ditch and enclose his ground, to manor and husband it as good farmers use' (pp. 134–35). Throughout *A View* Spenser suggests that the real motives in human conduct are not abstract ideas but economic interests. His book analyses historical events in terms of battles over property; the claims of the English to Ireland are based on right of conquest alone. Much of *A View* is concerned with the imposition of law on the colonised people, and Spenser is clear that human law has little to do with absolute morality: 'no laws of man, according to the strait rule of right, are just, but as in regard of the evils which they prevent and the safety of the commonweal they provide for' (p. 65). (We could try viewing Book 5 of *The Faerie Queene*, particularly Talus, in the light of this.) Abstract ideals have less force than material interests. Thus he explains corruption in the rule of Ireland, since governors have been motivated mainly by their own jealous self-protection rather than patriotism: 'some of them, seeing the end of their government to draw nigh, and some mischief or troublous practice growing up (which afterwards may work trouble to the next succeeding governor), will not attempt the redress or cutting off thereof, either for fear they should leave the

9

realm unquiet at the end of their government or that the next which cometh should receive the same too quiet—and so happily win more praise thereof than they before' (p. 144).

Physical force is the primary method of control, coming before religion: 'instruction in religion needeth quiet times, and ere we seek to settle a sound discipline in the clergy, we must purchase peace unto the laity, for it is ill time to preach amongst swords' (p. 138). And before law: 'For it is vain to prescribe laws where no man careth for keeping them nor feareth the danger for breaking them. But all the realm is first to be reformed and laws are afterwards to be made' (p. 147). I spell out this point about the primacy of economics and physical force because our picture of Spenser's thought has been so heavily influenced by numerous critical works that attend solely to the abstractions of, say, *The Faerie Queene*. We should perhaps attend afresh to the descriptive poetry's insistence on the physical bloodiness of the battles necessary to impose these moral values; and to the catalogue of bloodshed in the Book of Briton Monuments which Arthur reads (and which contrasts with Guyon's nice faery history book). It is, hence, significant that (as several critics have noted) Book 5, the Book of Justice, is the most poetically uneven, not to say muddle-headed; at its heart, the necessary split in the virtuous duo, between the inhuman physical force of the iron man Talus and the just-dealing Artegall, produces the contradictory idea that human justice is not alternative to, but dependent on, that which is inhuman.

The scepticism in *A View* is coupled with a sense of urgency. Spenser lived and worked on the colonial front-line. His book is a plea for a specific policy towards Ireland, but it also speaks more generally of the interrelationship of monarch, feudal overlords and gentlemen entrepreneurs. Repeatedly *A View* recommends breaking the power of the Irish overlords. It suggests the use of religion and law to loosen the control of the lords: 'I hold it no wisdom to leave

10

unto them too much command over their kindred, but rather to withdraw their followers from them as much as may be, and to gather them under the command of law' (p. 81). The analysis separates the 'base sort of people' from the 'grand rebels': 'all the rebellions which you see from time to time happen in Ireland are not begun by the common people but by the lords and captains of countries, upon pride or wilful obstinacy against the government' (p. 205). A system of law imposed by central government would function to break the traditional, local bonds of lord and followers. Independence from the lord can be marked both in society and in individual consciousness by naming:

> it was commanded, that whereas all men then used to be called by the name of their septs [clans] according to their several nations, and had no surnames at all, that from thenceforth each one should take unto himself a several surname, either of his trade and faculty, or of some quality of his body or mind, or of the place where he dwelt, so as every one should be distinguished from the other, or from the most part. Whereby they shall not only not depend upon the head of their sept, as now they do, but also shall in short time learn quite to forget his Irish nation. (p. 215)

Thus instead of feudal bonds, Irish tradition, national identity, the new naming will stress individual autonomy. And the new incentives will be economic: 'to appoint to every one that is not able to live off his freehold a certain trade of life, to which he shall find himself fittest and shall be thought ablest, the which trade he shall be bound to follow and live only thereupon' (p. 215). Against the power of the feudal lords new power will be given to 'corporate' and 'free' towns: 'not depending upon the service, nor under the command, of any but the governor.... they will both strengthen all the country round about them, which by their means will be the better replenished and enriched, and also

11

be as continual holds for Her Majesty' (p. 227). Spenser here invokes the model of the Low Countries, but he could have looked nearer home—at the corporate power of the City of London. For Spenser's commentary on the Irish social order has direct relevance to England.

The Tudor dynasty established its power by reducing the strength of other aristocratic families. It aspired in theory, if not in fact, to absolute monarchy. Thus the ideology of Tudor absolutism elevated the monarchical line by depicting the ruler not as a leader among other aristocrats but as a prince divinely appointed, magically special. This mystique justified and complemented what in reality underpinned it— an increasingly efficient administration. This administration used legal, religious and fiscal measures to sustain the monarch's power, instead of the old armed bands of aristocratic warlords. In addition to the use of religion and law to circumvent lords' power, Spenser cynically recommends taxation for noblemen: 'whom I would have thought to have been of so honourable minds as that they should not need such a base kind of being bound to their allegiance—who should rather have held in and stayed all others from undutifulness, than need to be forced thereunto themselves' (p. 204). Civil peace in England is attributed to the lack of power of overlords, who have no command 'because every man standeth upon himself and buildeth his fortunes upon his own faith and firm assurance' (p. 205).

That last point about individualism—every man standing upon himself—is the crucial step from the administration of the state to the conduct of the individual, from the body politic to the body private. We have seen how, to limit the lords' power, the Irish were to be individually named and given individual trades as both incentives to and reminders of their own individuality. This idea of individuality was, of course, male; it was the father's name and power that were passed on. The trade Spenser most recommends is husbandry, because it is necessary, easily learnt and opposed to warfare: 'husbandry, being the nurse of thrift and daughter of industry and labour, detesteth all that may work her scathe and destroy the travail of her hands' (p. 216) (we should note Spenser's image, which conceives of 'husbandry' as the domesticated woman servicing the active male qualities). By contrast, the 'keeping of cows is of itself a very idle life and a fit nursery for a thief' (p. 217). So the requirements of weakening the overlords and of profitably exploiting the colony produce a stress on the virtues of individual thrift and labour, discipline and hard work. It is in such virtues that the knights of *The Faerie Queene* are trained as they somewhat nominally serve their queen.

The problems for Spenser's text come with the definition of the monarchy which will limit the overlords and uphold individual effort. Arguing that all in Ireland is 'absolutely' the monarch's, it urges a strengthening of the centre of government. This serves the purpose of limiting the power of feudal lords and creating new sources of profit. But Spenser is at the same time careful to delimit the royal power in one notable instance: 'I do not think it convenient, though now it be in the power of the prince, to change all the laws and make new; for that should breed a great trouble and confusion, as well in the English there dwelling and to be planted, as also in the Irish' (p. 199). The discussion of Ireland here touches on an issue of major concern in England. Elizabeth had continued to develop the Tudor project to become absolute rulers. Hence she claimed a prerogative to make laws at will, by personal fiat. This was increasingly a contentious issue between monarch and parliaments. The opposition in Parliament argued that the queen was bound by the common law of the land, and that personal royal prerogative should have no power over that of Parliament. When MPs spoke their opposition to the crown they appealed to their individual consciences. Their

13

argument was similar to that used by Spenser against feudal overlords. We know also that Spenser admired the political theorist George Buchanan, who argued for a limited monarchy.

Spenser's caution in the passage above seems to show awareness of the debates around law and royal privilege. His flattery of the monarch, together with his assumption of her absolute right to Ireland, coexist with apparent criticism of her rule. He notes that the 'Arch-rebel' the Earl of Tyrone was encouraged by finding 'great faintness in her majesty's withstanding him' (p. 166). Indeed, the queen contributed to the power of the Earl when, as Baron of Dungannon, he 'was set up as it were to beard [Shane O'Neill], and countenanced and strengthened by the queen so far as that he is now able to keep herself play' (p. 167). This history of the English campaigns in Ireland shows that at crucial junctures the monarch either supported leading Irish overlords or fatally curtailed the powers of English war-leaders. Spenser gives an example of the first strategy; for the second we might note how limits were set on Essex's expedition in 1574, how Lord Deputy Sidney's colonial plans were hindered or overruled, how the formation of a garrison in Ulster was blocked, how the queen negotiated with Gaelic chiefs against the St Leger project in Munster.

These apparent contradictions in policy may be interpreted, again, by reference to the absolutist project. Tudor monarchs faced on one hand aristocratic families whose power came from traditional landed wealth, and on the other they were potentially challenged by gentry whose wealth derived from mercantile projects, investment and adventuring as much as from land. The gentry opposition is expressed in parliamentary debates and refusals to renew royal subsidies; the aristocratic rivalry may be seen in Leicester's fully equipped stronghold at Kenilworth and his acceptance of the governorship of the Netherlands. Both aristocrats and gentlemen entrepreneurs had designs on exploiting Ireland. Spenser's own solution, which highlights the role of the corporate towns, trade and labour, seems in line with the second group. His text clearly has its moments of frustration with a royal policy which fails to serve consistently their interests.

For Spenser there was something more deeply wrong than inconsistencies in policy. Ireland, like any colonised country, was a testing-ground for developing political and military practices which might eventually be useful in controlling opposition at home (as, in our times, the British police have for instance assimilated the techniques of viciousness of the Hong Kong force). English measures in Ireland were justified on the grounds that if Ireland were not suppressed, it would itself threaten England. But the testing-ground is also (always) a minefield. On the opening page of A View Spenser conjectures that god has kept Ireland 'in this unquiet state still, for some secret scourge which shall by her come unto England' (p. 44). As a bureaucrat of the occupying power, and even more as a settler, Spenser knew both that Ireland was a place of opportunity for the English landless ... and that it could destroy the settlers if it was not fully subdued. His poetic masterpiece tells of champions who barely overcome their opponents; and even that necessary fantasy pegs out with the humiliation of Artegall and the failure of Calidore fully to destroy the monster that threatened both of them.

In part the Irish threat was military. Spenser describes guerrillas who operate under cover of woodlands and wild areas. They perhaps enter his poetry in the images of dark, wild or tangled places which are associated frequently with evil. But more serious was the Irish potential to undermine the claim of the English to a superiority socially signified in their civility and education. Spenser frequently attacks the descendants of earlier English settlers, whose attitudes to and

15

relations with the Irish natives were often more liberal than those of the new wave of colonists. They are 'degenerated and grown almost mere Irish, yea and more malicious to the English than the very Irish themselves'. (Here, as elsewhere, Spenser writes as if there were no native Irish civilisation and culture; these were in fact destroyed by the English colonisers, whose activities were justified in part by such things as Spenser's scathing remarks about Irish bards as rabble-rousers.) The evidence of the English degeneration raises questions about the naturalness of racial superiority, and about the influence of environment and education on personal identity: 'Is it possible that an Englishman, brought up naturally in such sweet civility as England affords, can find such liking in that barbarous rudeness that he should forget his own nature and forego his own nation?' (p. 96). The problems around what Elizabethans called 'nurture' and 'nature' were of pressing importance in the business of empire-building. If *natural* superiority could not be demonstrated, then a major ideological justification of colonialism vanished.

Towards the end of his writing life Spenser was having problems with the concepts of nurture and civility. These are marked in Book 6 of *The Faerie Queene*. In the previous book, Artegall had to wage a series of campaigns against monstrous or overmighty enemies. The defensive or liberation battles had to be brutal and clear-cut. In the following Book there is an interest in how to maintain a civil society, and much of the action involves the knight of courtesy imposing civil standards on the less civilised. Calidore's superiority lies not in the demonstrable strength of his sword arm, but in his claim to 'grace'. And here Spenser's text cannot settle the nurture/nature dispute. The extended display of the impact of Calidore on a pastoral community suggests that his courtesy is simultaneously a form of management.

A *View* discounts the notion that English settlers brought 'civil fashions' to Ireland: 'the chiefest abuses which are now in that realm are grown from the English, and the English that were are now much more lawless and licentious than the very wild Irish' (p. 113). The degeneration of the English is caused not by nature but by the system of government itself. The governors who enforced the law tended to come from the great, but rival, families of Geraldines and Butlers who although 'very brave and worthy men' 'yet through greatness of their late conquests and seignories, they grew insolent and bent both that regal authority and also their private powers one against another, to the utter subversion of themselves and strengthening of the Irish again' (p. 114). The conquest which is so necessary can itself lead to failure and weakness: 'the English lords and gentlemen who then had great possessions in Ireland began, through pride and insolency, to make private wars one against another. And when either part was weak, they would wage and draw in the Irish to take their party, by which means they both greatly encouraged and enabled the Irish' (pp. 114–15). Although Spenser is again making the case against feudal overlords and in favour of a centralised administration, his description shows how the competition for property has a logic of its own. This logic calls into question the ideals of racial superiority and higher civility that supposedly justify colonialism. It is an analysis informed by the actual history of entrepreneurs in Ireland. For example, the activities of St Leger and his company were deliberately restrained by the Privy Council. But in this case, as in so many others, what was at stake was the power-contest between one class grouping and another, rather than ideals of civility. Spenser's argument implies that there is no civilising way of colonialism: the English 'are now grown to be almost as lewd as the Irish'. Then Spenser quickly adds: 'I mean of such English as were planted above toward the West' (p. 115). That addition reveals a difficulty

17

that goes all the way to the heart of A *View*.

The book seeks to outline a scheme for a stable and profitable occupation of Ireland. It has to concede, however, that a major obstacle is the corruption of the occupying force. Although this corruption is said to be a thing of the past, much of Spenser's analysis indicates that the problem is in the present. After all, Lord Deputy Sidney had been hindered and some of Elizabeth's policies had been crucially 'faint'. But the problem went deeper: in many ways the occupying power closely resembled the occupied. This might be shown trivially, in hair style: when Irenius attacks the Irish 'glib', he is told to take heed 'seeing our Englishmen take it up in such a general fashion to wear their hair so unmeasurable long that some of them exceed the Irish glibs' (p. 102). Or it may be more serious, as in religion: 'whatever disorders ye see in the church of England ye may find there, and many more, namely gross simony, greedy covetousness, fleshly incontinence, careless sloth, and generally all disordered life in the common clergymen' (p. 139). Likewise the system of wardships was attacked (p. 73).

A *View* resolves its difficulties by falling back on the idea of quintessential evil. So although the English have long hair, Irish glibs are different because of a 'savage brutishness and loathly filthiness' (p. 102). The disloyal alliance of earlier English settlers with the Irish is spoken of as a disease: 'the contagion thereof hath remained still amongst their posterities' (p. 117). The imagery works hard to produce ideas of natural, and contagious, evil, but the text has to guard against the suggestion that simply being in Ireland causes corruption. The topic is debated: 'Lord, how quickly doth that country alter men's natures. It is not for nothing I perceive which I have heard, that the Council of England think it no good policy to have that realm reformed or planted with English, lest they should grow as undutiful as the Irish and become much more dangerous'. 'Neither is it the nature of the country to alter men's manners, but the bad minds of the man' (pp. 210–11). A *bad* mind rejects English nurture and exploits the slack laws in Ireland, so that 'as it is the nature of all men to love liberty, so they become libertines and fall to all licentiousness of the Irish' (p. 211). The slip between liberty and libertine is very tricksy. In trying to suggest a difference in quality between liberty and licentiousness, the prose is trying to draw a line which in material terms does not exist. We might also ask about the value of English nurture, if it can always be rejected by a bad mind. Spenser's prose is in difficulties because it cannot openly admit that the Irish project itself corrupts. This would be to admit that the activity of colonising is always doomed to failure, since the colonisers' interest in their own economic advantages will (and did) outweigh their loyalty to central government. The very extension of English rule spawns a threat to that rule. Rather than think through that intolerable contradiction, Spenser's text suggests either that the English have 'caught' evil from the Irish or that some of them naturally have evil minds.

The intellectual trap derives from the problems inherent in feudal conquest. The carving-up of new lands, the establishment of corporate towns, give to the new landowners or enfranchised traders the sources of wealth which can in turn challenge the power of central government. For that central government is itself merely a landowner supported by a small administration and a myth of divinity. The realities of Spenser's often precarious existence as a settler in Ireland gave their own shape to his intellectual, and poetic, output. They brought to the fore both the necessities and fragilities of contemporary ideology.

The emergence of the political outlook represented by *A View* late in Spenser's life needs to be traced through his poetic writings. Before I do that, however, I want to juxtapose my account of Spenser here with the more traditional picture. My main source of reference is the 'official' biography by A. C. Judson, published in 1945. The first sentence of the biography notes the birth of Elizabeth Spencer of Althorp, Northamptonshire; the second sentence the birth of Edmund Spenser. By giving primary place to aristocratic Spencers, and to the poet's *possible* kinship with them, Judson plays down the fact of Spenser's lower-class birth. The inappropriateness of his class origin to his literary status is a problem for a number of critics. Thus Watson (1967) with a blithe notion of class says his father is both a 'gentleman' and a 'free journeyman'; and quickly quotes the claimed link with the Spencers of Althorp. This claim, as we shall see, is motivated by Spenser's own ambition, rather than being a statement of his real place in the world.

Like so many critics, Judson constructs for Spenser a sensibility appropriate to the role of great English poet. Describing his travels with Lord Grey, Judson tells us 'his antiquarian tastes would have been pleased by this ancient town ... he would have enjoyed the quiet beauty of its setting' (p. 89). This sensibility (based entirely on conjecture) is offered to us a couple of pages before Judson deals with Spenser's uncomplaining presence at the revolting massacre of Smerwick, at which, in November 1580, 600 already disarmed Italians and Spaniards were slaughtered. Spenser's own justification of that massacre is hard-headed and brutal, not at all sensitive and aesthetic. (Though in reality nothing hinders a lover of antiques from being an accessory to mass murder; indeed the two have often gone together. But that's not the effect Judson is after.) In his later assessment of Grey, Judson remarks that his success can never be settled 'unless to win the hearty approval of a man like Spenser can in itself be viewed as a kind of success' (p. 109). So not only does Spenser's sensibility raise him above the grubbier English brutalities, but association with his creativity is also capable of sanitising the butcher Grey.

As the biography reaches its end, the glorification of Spenser becomes the more conspicuous: 'Beauty for him was a ruling passion. He felt its magic in nature, in tapestry and armour and architecture, in man and especially in woman, and his Platonism gave him logical grounds for the reverence it inspired. Finally his love for his country must not be forgotten, nor for his queen as its symbol' (p. 212). We may set all of this alongside the text of A *View*, and we have to conclude that Judson is inventing his own fantasy version —appropriate for the mid–1940s—of what 'Spenser' ought to be. The importance of the patriotism may be measured when earlier Judson manages to liken the Irish rebels on Spenser's estate to the Nazi troops who invaded France. But alongside this and the (heterosexually defined) aesthetic sense may be set another fantasy: 'He gains learning, he founds a house, he acquires ... the reputation of being England's principal poet' (p. 210); ' "Rich" is a relative term and possibly should not be applied to him, but his success in gaining a competence appears to be at least comparable with Shakespeare's' (p. 211). The text implies that both artists are great not so much because of their art but because they can make money; and making money is a good thing. Spenser, like Shakespeare, was a successful social-climber. His artistic achievement is linked with a new class-position. What is envisaged is a glorious golden meritocracy where literary skills permit the innocent acquisition of wealth—a nice clean dream of tasteful bourgeois enterprise.

Judson's problem is that the fantasy won't work. In its attempt to be as complete as possible, the biography has to include all the grubby stories about Spenser's property deals. Judson remarks that in Spenser's years as deputy-clerk in Munster all the details of the resettlement project were known to him, 'hence his final acquisition of thousands of acres of forfeited lands was entirely natural' (p. 116). That word 'natural' is justifying a lot of crooked practice. He was

21

accused by his Anglo-Irish neighbour Lord Roche of falsely dispossessing the lord of castles and ploughlands, and of beating up the lord's servants and bailiffs. Spenser's answer does not deny this, but accuses Lord Roche of disloyalty and a series of isolated offences, including killing two beeves. Lord Roche did not get anything from Spenser at this time (though one Nicholas Shynan did get back two ploughlands granted to Spenser), but in 1595 two ploughlands were awarded to Roche in a second dispute and a commission inquired into the value of what Spenser had taken from these lands. At this point Judson desperately appeals to the account of the pastoral community in Book 6 of *The Faerie Queene* to show how Spenser really valued the peace of country life, beyond the litigations. But if we remember how the pastoral scene is exploited by Calidore's sexual interest, naively justified by the doomed Meliboe and easily disrupted by bandits, Judson's evidence turns back against him. A later attempt to appeal to poetry likewise breaks down: when Judson cites the opinion of the chief justice of Munster, William Saxey, that the office of sheriff of Cork was often filled by self-seeking men, he argues that the 'author of the Legend of Justice ... would have been an exception to the type depicted by Saxey' (p. 200). But, for many, the Legend of Justice is conspicuously a saga of brutality.

Spenser, with his friend Lodowick Bryskett (the Clerk of the Council of Munster), clearly benefited from the Irish land that was doled out to his followers by Lord Grey. Indeed Bryskett complained to Sir Francis Walsingham— Secretary of State and head of the secret service—when the queen tried to limit this outrageous carve-up. What is noticeable is that Spenser, the supposed lover of the country life, did not settle on the land leased to him. In December 1581, three days after a lease was granted him, he conveyed it to someone else. In the next three years he bought the lease on an old monastery at New Ross and again sold it. By 1582 he could write 'Gent' after his name, but he didn't try to become a settled landed gentleman as soon as he could. Instead he made a set of business deals over land-leases. During this period Spenser also leased the New Abbey (an old friary) in County Kildare, but after seven and a half years he forfeited the lease because he never paid his rent. It is an interesting reflection on Judson's method that while his main text invites us to 'imagine Spenser's wandering through the desolate choir ... and observing with admiration the beautiful central steeple of the decaying pile' (p. 103), the fact about the unpaid rent is consigned to a footnote. Clearly Spenser didn't want actually to pay for his beauties—if he found them beautiful at all. From the biography there emerges (albeit unintentionally) a picture of a Spenser who witnessed the trials and executions of great men, used his administrative office to pursue legal battles with resident lords, and did deals over ancient properties. This picture both connects with and illuminates the text of A View.

Spenser's social ascent was engineered through office-holding rather than through land-ownership. In 1583 and 1584 he was a commissioner of musters in County Kildare. There is a record of him holding a benefice at the parish of Effin in 1586. Such a benefice could be a source of income (Philip Sidney held several). But the record indicates that Spenser was delinquent in paying the required first year's income. Again it seems that, despite his poetic attacks on corruption in church livings, Edmund was on the fiddle. Furthermore his assumed loyalty to central government was limited by his financial interests. In May 1589 he refused to answer a government questionnaire as to how many Irish were on his estate (he was meant to be filling it with English, which was a harder, and more expensive, task). Three years later he omitted to provide a list of his tenants to a government commission, which was taken to be evidence of a failure in his project as estate-owner. And before we leave this topic, it is interesting to note that Elizabeth Boyle, the wife so romanticised by the *Amoretti*, was after his death accused by her stepson Sylvanus of withholding from him the title-deeds of Spenser's property at Kilcolman. Judson tries to keep Elizabeth innocent by blaming her second husband for the offence, but there's no proof. It looks as if sharp practice ran in the family.

Judson cannot be blamed too much. The manufacture of a sensitive poetic Spenser began even in the man's life. It was consolidated in John Milton's reference to the 'sage and serious' Spenser. And it has now become a major activity of the Spenser industry, as each new generation—including this book too—constructs an image of the artist which fits appropriately with the values of the critic's own time (though we should note, in passing, that W. B. Yeats, alongside all the sentimental mystification, says 'When Spenser wrote of Ireland he wrote as an official, and out of thoughts and emotions that had been organised by the State. He was the first of many Englishmen to see nothing but what he was desired to see.' 1902, p. 572). Tonkin (1972) tells us that the 'poem is like life'; A. C. Hamilton (1977), in his edition of *The Faerie Queene*, that the 'whole poem is deeply rooted in the human condition' (p. 23). And what view of life does 'Spenser' have? Tonkin says of 'the paradox of time and eternity': 'Behind this great central dilemma of the human condition stand lesser questions—man's conduct in society, the meaning of social order, the nature of human love.' ... The sorts of problems that concern anyone privileged enough not to have to worry about starvation. And the solution? Spenser's poem 'provides us with the mythic equipment to make our own resolutions, or to face their incompletenesses' (p. 113). Or as Evans (1970) has it, Spenser 'opposes to the stain of the Fall the profoundest human vision of truth' ... which is? 'the inspired vision of the poet' (p. 213). 'Spenser' is so convenient in offering myths and poems as social solutions rather than nasty measures like the redistribution of wealth. He is so nicely apolitical: 'the real bond of sympathy between Spenser and Sidney ... was their interest in the future of English letters' (Watson, 1967). But in a crisis 'Spenser' is still useful: 'he provides graphic evidence that man must never permit his civilization to render him incapable of defending himself against the enemies of that civilization' says Cheney (1966), writing during the escalation of the Vietnam War. In 1968 Dunseath pointed out that although the communist Giant's 'descendants are slowly winning the day in the twentieth century' Faery land is firmly conservative (p. 97); so student rioters can't enlist 'Spenser's' aid. Coles *Notes* (written by H. M. Priest, 1968) offers them straightforward patriotism: in Elizabeth's reign the 'Protestants were in and the Catholics out ... Most Englishmen had had enough of this [the no-nonsense chappies] ... Spenser, an ardent supporter of the Church of England [wrong! – but a patriotically well-intentioned error] ... wrote ... with unabashed partisan animus' [another sturdy English thing to do] (p. 9). In 1970 Renwick could justify Spenser's attitude to Ireland: 'That he did not imagine that English social and political ideals might not appeal to other peoples, only proves him a true Englishman'; for, anyway, Ireland is 'a country where human life has never been highly regarded' (does he mean by the British occupying forces in 1970? Renwick, 1970, pp. 188, 185).

But alongside the versions of the 'sage and serious', respectably English, image we must now set the upwardly mobile civil servant with his rent arrears and shady property deals. Spenser the Elizabethan yuppie. Who also wrote poems.

## B. Courts and Savages, and Vice Versa

Spenser's role as colonial official allowed him to change his status to that of gentleman-settler. In making that move, he became financially a little less dependent on central government, though he always relied for his landed security on the presence of English forces. As a poet, however, he had to look always towards the court for favour and rewards.

This section aims to pursue further the set of political ideas in their various manifestations in Spenser's poetry. There are, of course, shifts in emphasis since we are looking at a range of writing across about twenty years, but they don't substantially alter the general picture. The survey of political ideas begins with Spenser's contradictory response to central authority, a response which in *A View* may be seen to be both critical and dependent. Both aspects are marked clearly in his earliest major work, *The Shepheardes Calender*.

This poem has received a great deal of critical attention, so I shall not bother with detailed analyses which merely duplicate the efforts of others. We can say briefly that *The Shepheardes Calender* criticises corruption in the church and advocates the sort of low-church organisation and principles which would be associated with the more radical wing of puritanism. It specifically commends Edmund Grindal, the archbishop of Canterbury whom Elizabeth had dismissed in June 1577 because he refused to comply with her attempts to suppress puritan gatherings. We can note too that the poem makes a brief critique of the state: the 'October' eclogue claims that poetry is in decline because there is neither active virtue nor warrior prowess to praise; and nobody to patronise poets. It is made clear that since 'Princes pallace' is the 'most fitt' to patronise poetry, this is a specific failure of the ruler. 'October' carefully directs itself to a central authority without specifying who rules:

Whither thou list in fayre Elisa rest,
Or if thee please in bigger notes to sing,
Advaunce the worthy whome shee loveth best,
That first the white beare to the stake did bring.

(45-48)

The 'worthy', as the coat of arms indicates, is Leicester; the problem is in what sense the notes that praise him need to be 'bigger' than those that praise Elizabeth, and why. At the time of writing of this poem, Leicester had considerable personal power backed up by military force and networks of patronage. More than being a source of money and promotion, Leicester's patronage and leadership had a specific ideological identity. He was seen as leader by many sections of the puritan movement, and many gentlemen entrepreneurs aligned themselves with him. In crude terms, the Leicester grouping supported an aggressive foreign policy in which England placed itself at the head of the Protestant nations against Catholic regimes (these were the 'super-power' blocs between which Europe was divided). Such a position led to explicit criticism of the queen (whose policies were less aggressive). In the year of publication of *The Shepheardes Calender* Elizabeth was heavily criticised for contemplating marriage to the French Duke d'Alencon. Sidney, who was closely identified with—and related to—the Leicester faction, had to go into provincial exile as a result of his writing to the queen a letter critical of the proposed marriage; and for writing a similar text, the puritan pamphleteer Philip Stubbes (1543?-1591), not being a gentleman, had his right hand chopped off. Spenser's poem makes his alignment plain through the series of names he invokes: praise for the puritan Grindal (thinly disguised in the anagram 'Algrind'), elevation of Leicester through his coat of arms (which one of the poem's notes teasingly exploits: 'being not likely, that the names of noble princes be

27

known to country clowne'), dedication to Sidney 'most worthy of all titles' (which must have looked ironic by the end of 1579), and printed by Hugh Singleton, who was famous for printing puritan tracts. It doesn't need the poet's name on the text for it to be explicitly placed within a cultural and political grouping.

We don't know why Spenser didn't put his name to the text; some people suggest that he was following a social convention by which gentlemen did not publish, or did not own to publishing, their writings. Certainly the absence of a name causes post-structuralist delight, since *The Shepheardes Calender* can be said to have a series of 'authors'; whether it be Immerito, who writes the envoy; or Colin, who is the central poet figure in the narrative; or the supposed 'editor' EK, who seems so privy to the author's intentions (and whose identity is itself so mysterious and disputed); or the maker of the woodcuts, which themselves work as commentaries. And none of these authors has a discernable real-life existence. The appearance of the 'new poet' is the appearance not of an individual with a text in which he expresses himself but the appearance of a text created by a group of (fictional) authors. The anonymity is fruitfully developed by the text into a series of questions about authorial identity, authorial intention and creative expression. Yet we should not assume it was only a game. Spenser may have felt it was politic to keep the text anonymous; the new poet was hedging his bets. His more overtly political poem produced (in part) in this period, *Mother Hubberds Tale*, was not printed but circulated in manuscript. The strength of its material may be measured by the fact that when it was printed ten or so years later it was 'called in' by the censors. Indeed that event earned for Spenser a reputation somewhat different from that of the 'sage and serious' so often reproduced by contemporary critics. The satirist and dramatist Thomas Middleton, whose own works were often overtly political, remarked in 1604 that *Mother Hubberd* was called in for 'selling her working bottle-ale to bookbinders, and spurting the froth upon courtiers' noses' (the image stresses the volatile contents of the poem); and in 1615 Thomas Scot wrote:

> If Spencer now were living, to report
> His *Mother Hubberts* tale, there would be sport:
> To see him in a blanket tost, and mounted
> Up to the Starrs.
> (quoted in *Minor Poems 2, Variorum*, p. 582)

It was very soon after the distribution of both these poems that Spenser left the relatively secure service of Leicester for Ireland. We can't know if the prospect of economic gain outweighed his poetic ambitions, or if the very poetry he had written made it necessary to leave the country. Perhaps the two motives coincided; perhaps it was not his decision anyway.

*The Shepheardes Calender* is very much more than a text which participates in the factional politics of the Elizabethan state. Many modern commentaries have emphasised the poem's interests in rhetoric, poetry writing and the 'inner life' of the poet. In turn, these interests may be related to the poem's relationship with the political figures who patronise poetry or the religious and social debates which employ rhetoric for political effect. The opening eclogue concentrates on the image of the alienated poet, given pride of place in the text written by an aspiring poet. Government of self and flock, sexual desire and frustration, poetic skill, expression and patronage are all linked together. It should be stressed that the poem remains a political poem, but it invites readers to extend their idea of the 'political'.

The complexity of the response produced in the reader relates to Spenser's own contradictory position. Both may be

demonstrated from the 'February' eclogue. A story about
an oak and a briar is told as part of a debate between youth and
age. Story and debate are linked in an ironic way: old age
uses rhetoric even while he condemns it, youth is not
impressed by the moral story, the generation battle itself ties
in with Spenser's own perceived position as a new young
writer in a society which stressed conservatism and order
(see Montrose, 1981). Although the story is supposedly told
to make a moral point, its language encourages a political
reading. As well as the oak being grey and bald, his 'honor' is
decayed. The briar is 'bragging', but also its flowers are white
and red 'Colours meete to clothe a mayden Queene' (132).
White and red flowers can be generally associated with
courtly poetry, but specifically perhaps with the Tudor rose:
the colours reappear to grace Elisa in 'Aprill', as does the
'mayden Queene' phrase. When the husbandman appears,
the briar addresses him as 'my soveraigne', 'placer of plants,
both humble and tall' (163–64). The husbandman as a
human has authoritative, monarchical status. Nevertheless
he is susceptible to the briar's rhetoric and to his own rage.
He chops down the oak, an error marked by the axe seeming
'halfe unwilling to cutte the graine' (204). The oak is not just
old, but holy: 'And often crost with the priestes crewe'
(209). But such rituals were 'foolerie'; EK links them to the
'popishe priest' and ancient 'blindnesse', which contribute to
the oak's 'decay', or 'miserye' as the narrator says. The oak
falls with a quaking of the ground, leaving the briar standing
'like a Lord alone'; but when winter comes the briar begins
to 'repent his pryde', and collapses. The restatement of the
moralistic terms apparently rounds off the tale, but it's a
false satisfaction. There are questions still open: the oak's
holiness is of a sort that is associated with ignorance, and
surely deserves to fall? When does the husbandman learn
not to make mistakes, and is he punished?

The apparent moral status of the story blurs its

connections with political issues, and its exemplary morality conceals problems. The method of the story sets up points of authority and dignity which are undercut. It is difficult for the reader to take sides; the oak's holiness is 'foolerie'; the husbandman is a 'good man' whose action kills both plants. Much critical writing, however, has attempted to 'clarify' the story by relating it to personalities in Elizabeth's court, and hence has suggested where we should 'really' sympathise. These attempts are frustrated responses to the method of the narrative. That method is dialectical, in that it takes the reader through an argument between forces which are opposed but mutually dependent. The husbandman, with his power and destruction, is a key to the action yet cannot be accounted for within the moral terminology. The reader's and commentator's distress is produced by the method, and that method is integral to the political vision. We are given a model of a dominant structure which is always in tension within itself, with its old order—the ignorant, vulnerable oak —and its emergent power—the flattering, temporarily successful briar. The monarch has power, but doesn't necessarily use it correctly. We are not offered a point of identification within this dominant order; the story's language engages our concern for its squabbles, its method alienates us from its contradictions. Furthermore as fiction it permits Spenser an escape from the difficulty of his own political insight: since the husbandman's action leaves the flimsy briar like a lord, only the arrival of winter brings it down. But to what political force does winter correspond? This question is unanswered. The story is ended and our attention is deflected from the reality of wrong-headed royal action—to which there's no apparent solution.

Against this alienated view of a complete dominant order, with monarch, residual and emergent forces all interrelated, may be placed the 'Aprill' eclogue. This singles out the monarch as an independent entity, and evokes the

31

mythology and propaganda rather than the power-relations of Elizabeth's rule. The famous hymn to Eliza offers the reader a single unfolding vision rather than dialectical complexity. The poetic pleasures derive from the harmony engendered by rhyme and alliteration, and from the accumulation of colours, mythic figures, flowers. The language of Elizabeth-worship is not alienated, as it is with the briar, and so perceived to function within power-relations. Instead that language performs its required ideological task by promising the reader (poetic) harmony and (poetic) acquisition. The reader—who is assumed, crucially, to be male—is given a position of power which is constructed from the idea of viewing. A woman is decorated by a male text and looked at by a male readership as an object. The male poet's skill brings into being this decorated woman. The (male) reader consents to imagine and respond to the poet's vision. (I should observe here that the position for the female reader is going to be more complex, although Spenser doesn't acknowledge this. As a male I can't know how this response works; my guess, at a minimum, is that for the heterosexual woman reader the pressure to appreciate the female sex objects constitutes one of the alienating features of Spenser's work. I very much look forward to the observations of women students specifically engaged in projects concerned with reading Spenser as women.) This makes the reader, by proxy, part of the power that brings this woman into being, to be looked at. To rhyme 'Maiestie' with 'modest eye' clinches it: the modest eye does not look back when it is looked at. The Majesty is subject to the gaze, and its value subject to the assent, of the reader; 'Where have you seene the like, but there?' (72).

Although pleasurable, this reader's position is clearly false. The hymn does not exhibit the language of Elizabethan myth, it employs its power. But the hymn is framed, and several clever commentaries have analysed the relationship of frame and hymn, as well as the language of the hymn itself. In brief, the hymn has been written by a poet whose 'mynd was alienate', and it is sung by his former but now rejected friend. While the text of the hymn celebrates fullness, its creator and performer are both frustrated and distressed. The glorification of Elisa/Elizabeth need not presuppose the contentment of the glorifiers. Hobbinol in fact sings to celebrate the skill of the absent Colin. The pleasurable vision of the absent Elisa is brought into being as a tribute to the absent Colin. After all its ideological workings, Hobbinol reminds us of the real power-relations: Colin is a fool 'That loves the thing, he cannot purchase' (159).

At a later date, when Spenser was more established in his career and social position, he returned to his early persona in order to write a version of his autobiography (it was also the time at which he probably finished his *View of Ireland*). *Colin Clouts Come Home Again* gives a picture of Spenser's relationship with central government; but the text's descriptions are themselves shot through with more contradictions. Colin tells why, although he had been rewarded there, he left the court:

> Happie indeed (said Colin) I him hold,
> That may that blessed presence still enjoy,
> Of fortune and of envy uncomptrold,
> Which still are wont most happie states t'annoy:
> But I by that which little while I prooved:
> Some part of those enormities did see,
> The which in Court continually hooved,
> And followd those which happie seemd to bee.
>
> (660–67)

Fortune and envy are tactfully vague ways of explaining why the presence may not be enjoyed, nor are the 'enormities' clarified here. We would expect the royal presence to be the continuity, the always-present, beyond the misfortunes of courtiers. But the lines insist on other continuities: fortune and envy 'still' control, enormities 'continually' remain alongside the 'blessed presence'. Cynthia rules over something which alienates simple shepherds:

> For sooth to say, it is no sort of life,
> For shepheard fit to lead in that same place,
> Where each one seeks with malice and with strife,
> To thrust downe other into foule disgrace,
> Himself to raise: and he doth soonest rise
> That best can handle his deceitfull wit,
> In subtil shifts, and finest sleights devise,
>
> (688–94)

The competition goes on despite the monarch, and the particular goal is social ascent *through one's own efforts*: this is emphasised and specified by the midway line-break (692). Colin's response to the corruption is to return to his sheep, claiming 'I silly man, whose former dayes/Had in rude fields bene altogether spent,/ Durst not adventure such unknowen wayes' (668–70). The traditional pastoral contrast of innocent rural stability against corrupt courtly 'unknowen wayes' invents a virtuous biography for Colin. Yet he also responds less passively when he claims that haughty courtiers are 'like bladders blowen up with wynd,/That being prickt do vanish into noughts (717–18). The text leaves open the question of who will do the pricking.

Colin is asked to except from his criticisms 'Lobbin' (the Earl of Leicester) and the nobility at court in his day. Some of these still remain, so Colin is unjust to blame everyone for what 'thou mislikedst in a few'. But Colin insists the majority is proud, envious and idle. The narrative at this point replaces one critique of the court with another. The first was based on a contrast between poor and rich, where the court was seen as competitive throughout and hence corrupt. This analysis is intolerable because Spenser has to concede his powerlessness in the face of it. The truth-speaking authority given to the persona is irrelevant to such established wealth-division. The second court-critique is more tolerable because it respects personal affiliations with the powerful and operates on moral, rather than economic, discrimination. It suggests that Spenser once had an entry to court through the Leicester faction, and hence that it need not be seen as uniformly corrupt in its very structure *as court*, but merely as a mixed group of good and bad courtiers. One critique of court happily cancels out the other.

Before leaving Spenser's views on courts, it may be worth noting that his antipathy is also to be found in *The Faerie Queene*. It is common nowadays to contrast the 'personal' focus of the first three Books with the 'social' focus of the others, which also show a developing bitterness. But this model seems both simple and sentimental (it comfortingly affirms that even the Spensers of this world get fed up with authoritarian government). In fact some of the clearest anti-court writing comes in Book 1 of *The Faerie Queene*, which we may guess to have been worked on soon after *The Shepheardes Calender*. In Canto 4 the Redcross knight arrives at the House of Pride, 'The house of mightie Prince it seemd to bee' (4.2): a magnificent building constructed without mortar and with thin walls covered in gold foil. Inside it is full of 'rich array and costly arras' (6); but 'the hinder parts, that few could spie,/ Were ruinous and old, but painted cunningly' (5). The structure is not merely insecure, but is a planned deception; it is a fiction of authority. Its economic effects are nevertheless real:

> Great troupes of people traveild thitherward
> > Both day and night, of each degree and place,
> > But few returned, having scaped hard,
> > With balefull beggerie, or foule disgrace,      (3)

35

These ruining effects are stated early on, so the wealthy
house never seduces the reader. Thus magnificence is always
seen to be corrupt, insecure and dangerous. The tone of
moral satire allows Spenser to be politically bold, while
appearing only to be moral. The Prince of this house is 'A
mayden Queene', very beautiful, dressed in gold and
precious stones. She is a snob and a usurper, without 'native
soveraintie':

> Ne ruld her Realmes with lawes, but pollicie,
> And strong advizement of six wisards old,
> That with their counsels bad her kingdome did uphold.(12)

The figure, in moral allegory, is Pride, and the six advisers
are other deadly sins. But pictures of beautiful maiden
queens have other reverberations in Elizabethan England,
and we ought to note that from the late 1570s many thought
the queen was trying to rule by prerogative and Privy
Council rather than with law made in Parliament. The
general anti-court satire here is as firmly pointed towards a
specific regime as anything in *The Shepheardes Calender*.

The alternative to this corruption is concentrated in the
Redcross knight. Before he leaves the House of Pride he
looks at a dungeon his dwarf has found. The majority of
those he sees

> Fell from high Princes courts, or Ladies bowres,
> Where they in idle pompe, or wanton play,
> Consumed had their goods, and thriftlesse howres,
>                                                           (5.51)

Again there is a transition: these lines tend to blame wasteful
people rather than inherently corrupt institutions. As such
they are relevant to the particular mission of Redcross,
whose individual project it is to learn the correct self-
discipline which will prepare him to fight the dragon. That

fight will take place outside the context of courts. Thus the narrative suggests that social problems may be solved by individual effort and self-control. The corruption of court is a transitory affair. In this way the narrative inverts the real situation, in which court is both powerful and permanent, and as such provides a fantasy that is pleasurable and necessary to those who distrust what they depend on.

A similar, but more advertised, shift occurs with Belphoebe's critique of courts:

> Who so in pompe of proud estate (quoth she)
>      Does swim, and bathes himselfe in courtly blis,
>      Does waste his dayes in darke obscuritee,
>
>                                              (2.3.40)

She says that only 'painfull toile' obtains honour, and 'Before her gate high God did Sweat ordaine' (41). After saying that the way is easy to 'pleasures pallace' the next stanza commences: 'In Princes court, The rest she would have said,' ... but she is interrupted (42). The interruption so early in the stanza calls attention to what might but cannot be said about princes' courts. The critique of courts is itself apparently irrelevant to the narrative action of Braggadocchio's lust for Belphoebe. But the interruption has a precise place: Belphoebe is an acknowledged figure for the queen; the queen's power was most often represented in the imagery and conventions of courtly devotion and loving service to a beautiful but chaste woman. Belphoebe is Elizabeth insofar as she is supremely beautiful and supremely chaste. But far from creating the supposed order, this beauty here provokes lust and disorder. The very apparatus which should stabilise monarchy produces a challenge to it. Here Spenser's critique of court combines with his masculine antipathy to female rulers (which we shall look at in the next chapter). The lust of Braggadocchio replaces Belphoebe's

37

commentary on princes' courts just as it is about to begin, and in fact serves as a better commentary—on a specific court.

On this subject I should observe that in general Spenser's heroes operate in ways that run counter to received notions of courtly behaviour or 'civil conversation'. For example, handbooks on courtesy suggested rules for appropriate styles of social conduct (see Whigham, 1984): the courtier would carefully observe trivial niceties while appearing to be spontaneous; he would demur about his own abilities while always really pushing himself, treat his apparent play as serious work. On the other hand Spenser's heroes have actually to *work* at their quests; they advance their causes by physical effort; they distrust courtly behaviour. To Britomart the six brothers 'traynd in all civilitee' are 'but shadowes' (3.1.44,45); reality is the questing spirit and the questing action. The heroes do not employ appropriate conduct to signify their rank in society; they make their place and achieve their goals by fighting for them. In the courtesy book it is seen as dangerous and vulnerable to be solitary, whereas Spenser's heroes have to be proved as individuals. Where he does recommend civil conversation, in *A View*, Spenser sees it as a form of training for the Irish which will make them submissive; it is an explicitly political tool.

When he wrote *A View* Spenser was fully implicated in the system which he was aspiring to join at the time he produced *The Shepheardes Calender*. The transition affects his broad political outlook. This may be shown in a brief comparison of religious views. In *The Shepheardes Calender* there is an attack on idolatry: Thomalin looks back to a time of simple religion of lowly shepherds, the hills

> I reverence and adore:
> Not for themselfe, but for the sayncts,
> Which han be dead of yore.
> (Julye, 114–15)

And Piers tells a moral tale of a fox disguised as a peddlar 'Bearing a trusse of tryfles at hys backe,/ As bells, and babes, and glasses in hys packe' (Maye, 239–40). Through most of *The Faerie Queene* Catholicism and high Anglicanism are associated with idols, rich vestments, and such religious bric-à-brac as rosaries and mitres. But at the end of Book 6 Calidore pursues the Blatant Beast to 'sacred Church' which it wrecks:

> And Altars fouled, and blasphemy spoke,
> And th' Images for all their goodly hew,
> Did cast to ground, whilest none was them to rew;
> (6.12.25)

And towards the end of *A View* we may recall that Spenser recommends repairing ruined churches to 'draw the rude people to the reverencing and frequenting thereof—whatever some of our late too-nice fools say, that there is nothing in the seemly form and comely order of the Church' (p. 223).

The older Spenser recommends the 'reverencing' that Thomalin had attacked. The 'too-nice fools' probably refers to radical puritan critics of church furnishings and fabric. In *The Shepheardes Calender* Spenser wrote from that critical position, but in *A View* he wants to preserve the appearances of churches because they play their part in controlling common people. The author of *A View* had a house and land threatened by the unrest of a native population. The author of *The Shepheardes Calender* was a student intellectual without, yet, a fixed place in the dominant order. Furthermore Spenser's writing life spanned the period of state repression of puritanism: it was strong in the 1570s but from the mid-1580s systematically subjected to the usual state techniques of show trials and executions, propaganda, censorship and torture. When Leicester died in 1588,

Spenser lost a figurehead; on a wider scale, puritanism lost a highly placed patron.

Against this shift must be placed a more consistent attitude to the church. In *The Shepheardes Calender* there are continual assaults on wealthy clergymen, those who are clad in 'purple and pall' and 'lord it, as they list' (Julye, 173 ff.). In 'Maye', Piers locates the corruption in the Anglican church with what is taken to be a reference to Wolsey:

> Some gan to gape for greedie governaunce,
> And match them selfe with mighty potentates,
> Lovers of Lordship and troublers of states:
>
> (121–23)

EK's note is interestingly cautious: 'Nought here spoken as of purpose to deny fatherly rule and godly governaunce ... but to displaye the pride and disorder of such, as in steede of feeding their sheepe, indeede feede of theyr sheepe' (p. 440). The note simultaneously detaches itself from radical critiques of church structure and restates the attack on corrupt individuals. Many puritans knew that individual abuses were permitted precisely by the structure of the Anglican church, but EK's note performs the (ideological) job of separating the two critiques.

The Priest in *Mother Hubberds Tale* tells the Fox and Ape that it is easy to make a successful career in the church. He says of 'Clerks'

> Is not that name enough to make a living
> To him that hath a whit of Natures giving?
> How manie honest men see ye arize
> Daylie thereby, and grow to goodly prize?
>
> (417–20)

The life is luxurious: 'Ne to weare garments base of wollen twist,/But with the finest silkes us to aray' (460–61). In A

*View* Spenser notes the financial corruption of the Irish bishops, who use their servants and horseboys to collect tithes with which they buy lands and build castles. The priests do not want to 'be drawn forth from their warm nests and their sweet loves' sides, to look out into God's harvest, which is even ready for the sickle and all the fields yellow long ago' (p. 222).

Although the attitude to religious display may change, the attack on the wealth and grandeur of churchmen remains consistent. The clue to Spenser's view lies both in the picture of churchmen who won't harvest their crops and in Piers's accusation that churchmen are 'Lovers of Lordship': a bad church is one which obtains wealth without working and meddles in state affairs. Throughout the feudal period much anti-clericalism was motivated at all levels by envy of the church's wealth, land and power. Popular discontent with exploitative priests was mobilised by secular lords to further their own designs on church power. Spenser's apparently complex religious position becomes more clear if seen not in theological but in economic terms. Here are three examples:

First: before the Blatant Beast pillages the church, it breaks into the monks' quarters,

> And searched all their cels and secrets neare;
> In which what filth and ordure did appeare,
> Were yrkesome to report; yet that foule Beast
> Nought sparing them, the more did tosse and teare,
> (6.12.24)

The detail of the 'filth and ordure' comes from a tradition of anti-monasticism based on jealousy of monastic wealth: it is expressed in attacks on the personal lives of 'decadent' monks. While the Beast is itself 'foule', it shows the filth that is in monasteries. The stanza can refuse to 'report' because readers could imagine the filth from their already learnt anti-

41

monastic prejudice. But it acts the pose of distaste. By contrast the next stanza, when the Beast desecrates 'sacred Church', asks the reader to 'rew' the damage—because no one else is around to do so. The text has it both ways: it attacks monasteries, but then asks the reader to sorrow for an act of desecration of what is sacred. Spenser resents the wealth, but by this stage he also politically valued the awe which religion could inspire.

Second: immediately before his attack on idle Protestant ministers in A View Spenser notes the enterprise of Catholics who come 'by long toil and dangerous travel hither, where they know peril of death awaiteth them and no reward or riches is to be found, only to draw the people unto the Church of Rome' (pp. 221–22). This admiration sits oddly beside the warnings in The Shepheardes Calender about foxes and wolves (covert Catholics and Jesuit spies) who undermine the English church. But the fox sought to trap the kid by trickery and charms; the Catholics in Ireland work. Consistent between the two texts is a valuing of work and enterprise. And I might add that uppermost in Spenser's mind in A View is not so much religious principle as the function of religion as a means of keeping populations docile.

Third, and in summary: early in The Faerie Queene, in the Book in which Redcross learns that true holiness means self-denial, discipline and permanent caution, Una—the true church—almost encounters Kirkrapine, a thief,

> Wont to robbe Churches of their ornaments,
> And poore mens boxes of their due reliefe,
> Which given was to them for good intents;
> The holy Saints of their rich vestiments
> He did disrobe, when all men carelesse slept,
> And spoild the Priests of their habiliments,
> Whiles none the holy things in safety kept;
> (1.3.17)

In the greater part of the Book rich vestments and ornament are associated with the false church in the person of Duessa. The stanza condemns Kirkrapine for stealing both poor boxes and religious ornament. It does not notice the contradiction (which *The Shepheardes Calender* remarks) between the charitable function of the church and its own wealthy fabric. It is more interested in urging the need for perpetual caution in order to protect the assets of the church. When the church is conspicuously exploited for personal gain and corrupt practices, it loses its function as an apparatus for social control, a function that operates by exhibiting charity and manufacturing mystery. The project of the greater part of the whole Book is to show the development and power of the true reformed church. Within this perspective, religious mumbo-jumbo and ornament are a bad thing. Thus this stanza seems somewhat inconsistent in its lament over vestments. But the inconsistency has occurred because Spenser has become temporarily engaged with questions of the economic and social place of the church as institution. His views here may therefore diverge from the religious principles enunciated by the rest of this particular Book; but they fall precisely into line with his attitude throughout his works.

The Spenser who wrote *A View* found it necessary to dismiss radical religious views as those of 'too-nice fools', even if he once held them himself. By this stage he had economic investments that made him more interested in stability than change. He remained critical of the wealth of clerics and the corruption of courts. But he depended for his own material security on a central government run by a monarch in conjunction with courtiers and rich churchmen. He was committed to an economic programme that valued individual enterprise and the marketing of goods, and which was expressed in ideological terms as a morality of discipline, forethought and hard work. Not being born into a landed inheritance himself, this was the only programme which allowed him to develop a personal career. But he had no manufacturing skill nor trading experience, no base for producing material wealth. He was an intellectual who could sell his services, not simply as poet, but as secretary, administrator and bureaucrat. Until he owned his own estate he was always looking to be employed by others, and whether or not he died in poverty his career never seemed to be financially successful nor economically secure.

In A View Spenser acknowledges that he is not himself an adventuring entrepreneur, but an administrator (at least that is the view of himself he prefers). His desire for strong rule relates to a need for peace and security. But because of the social contradictions endemic to an absolutist state, central government never guaranteed a consistency of rule which suited him. It both reduced the power of feudal overlords and then formed alliances with them against entrepreneurial gentry. For Spenser, therefore, great men and leaders were perilously close to destroyers and barbarians.

This is the picture of great men in A View. An example of the corruption of the earlier English settlers in Ireland is 'the great Mortimer who, forgetting how great he was once in England (or English at all), is now become the most barbarous of them all' (p. 117). These sorts of change in behaviour are explained by Irenius who is in 'inward trouble of mind to see her majesty so abused by some whom they put in special trust of those great affairs. Of which some, being martial men, will not do always what they may for quieting of things, but will rather wink at some faults and suffer them unpunished: lest they, having put all things in that assurance of peace that they might be, should seem afterwards not to be needed nor continued in their government with so great a charge to her majesty' (pp. 143–44). The transformation of leader into corrupt operator is brought about by the motive for power and profit. Spenser gives a materialist explanation, and twist, to an observation earlier made by Thomas Elyot, himself following Machiavelli, that the reverence for great men is both 'pleasant and terrible' (see Whigham, 1984, p. 64). Spenser's twist is that the opposed qualities of civility and savagery are not merely liabilities of service, but are placed within the great man as a social being.

The duality of great man/barbarian may clarify some of the problems thrown up by the imagery in *The Faerie Queene*. A number of people, in particular Berger (1957), have explained the apparent inconsistencies in the epic similes. Here I want to emphasise the element of contradiction. Before I do so, I should clarify the status of these similes. Some academics say that Spenser was simply imitating the sort of moral slipperiness of similes that appeared in Homer, but that explanation dodges the issue. We have to ask why Spenser bothered to use the simile in the same way (if at all); and what is significant about the places where he chooses to introduce a simile; and what *specific* values are blurred in a simile. (It should be added that there is ongoing debate among scholars of ancient Greek about the origin and function of these Homeric similes, so if we say that Spenser was consciously imitating them, are we sure he had the same idea about the definition of the thing he was imitating as we do?)

First let's see the fight between Calidore and Crudor (my view of this differs slightly from Whigham, 1984, p. 79):

> Thus long they trac'd and traverst to and fro,
>> And tryde all waies, how each mote entrance make
>> Into the life of his malignant foe;
>> They hew'd their helmes, and plates asunder brake,
>> As they had potshares bene; for nought mote slake
>> Their greedy vengeaunces, but goary blood,
>> That at the last like to a purple lake

45

> Of bloudy gore congeal'd about them stood,
> Which from their riven sides forth gushed like a flood.
>
> (6.1.37)

Each is a 'malignant foe' and both have 'greedy vengeaunces': the adjectives permit a blurring of good and bad, and the two supposed opposites become fused into one. The dominant logic of the passage is focused in the process of splitting open a pot to release its liquid contents. The stanza, aided by the well-placed alliteration, the repetition 'goary blood' 'bloudy gore' and the metrical fullness of the final alexandrine, builds to the final word 'flood'. Thus it is the mechanism of blood release rather than the contrast of moral opposites which provides the logic—and pleasure—of the stanza. Hero becomes inseparable from enemy.

There is a more pronounced moral dissolve in the epic similes, which anyway tend to complicate rather than clarify the actions they describe. When Artegall returns from saving Irena at the end of Book 5 he is confronted by Detraction and Envy, envisaged as two hags. This moment is taken to be Spenser's angry account of the 'unfair' blame which followed Lord Grey's (murderous) achievements in Ireland. Our knowledge of Spenser's sympathies tends to shape our reading of the description, which is itself pretty slippery:

> They both arose, and at him loudly cryde,
> As it had bene two shepheards curres, had scryde
> A ravenous Wolfe amongst the scattered flockes.
>
> (5.12.38)

Placing Artegall as 'wolf', the simile reverses the moral status of hero who should be guardian of the flock. A whole set of questions is triggered by the mismatch of simile and narrative: on what terms is Artegall/Grey 'wolf'? who are the flocks? why are they 'scattered'? what are Envy and

Detraction guarding? who is the shepherd? and why is s/he absent?

We can't clear up this mess by appealing to what Spenser 'intended', since the relationship between poetic intention and text has been demonstrated over the years to be highly unstable; nor can we simply say that the text is an autonomous entity with its own inconsistencies which clever readers can enjoy spotting. The text, even with its muddles and inconsistencies, has been produced by a real poet at a real time in history. We cannot account fully for that poet's own understanding of his historical circumstances, but we know it would have been (as for most people) complex. For the historical circumstances are shot through with contradictions so deep they are difficult to grasp. The specific nature of the complexity and the precise difficulties which he could not perhaps fully think through are illustrated in textual passages which show signs of inconsistency or confusion. Their muddle has a meaning which a reader can understand even if it eluded the poet.

To explain the hostility to Grey Spenser has to invent the figures of Envy and Detraction. The simile apparently suggests that Grey's activities might not be wholly advantageous to some sections of English home or colonial society. Spenser was witness to Grey's brutality, and conscious of it as a problem since he felt the need to defend it in A View. The text attempts to say Grey's enemies are motivated by an inexplicable malice, an evil which is not socially caused but is inherent and personal, such as envy in the abstract. But in the simile the text knows that this accusation is not quite satisfactory, things are left unsaid. The hero is, again, an unstable category.

Another example is Arthur's defeat of the Souldan, an allegory of the defeat of the Spanish Armada. In the narrative Arthur runs away from the Souldan; his only weapon is not force of arms but a mirror-like shield. The horses of the

Souldan are blinded by the shield and thus carry him to destruction. As readers we are engaged not so much with Arthur's efforts as with the Souldan's progress to his end, which consists of ,being torn apart when the chariot overturns. A simile follows:

> Like as the cursed sonne of Theseus,
>> That following his chace in dewy morne,
>> To fly his stepdames loves outrageous,
>> Of his owne steedes was all to peeces torne,
>> And his faire limbs left in the woods forlorne;
>> That for his sake Diana did lament,
>> And all the wooddy Nymphes did wayle and mourne.
>> (5.8.43)

This is not jingoistic Armada literature. The Souldan is compared to the tragic classical figure of Hippolytus, who was not to blame for his stepmother's passion. This link develops the tragic aspect of the Souldan's downfall in a chariot he can no longer control: a story of overweening might brought low by the source of its own power. The simile then provides the appropriate tragic reaction in the mourning of the nymphs; it invokes pity for the 'fair limbs' which are substituted for the image of the Souldan's body in its armour of 'bloodie rust' (29). The next stanza says the Souldan's death is an example of how justice brings down the mighty, but that example is no longer so clear. Spenser would surely have known the rhetoric of the Armada victory, which claimed that God helped the brave little English, but he produces instead an image of classic tragedy and mythological sorrow. The narrative is so handled that Arthur, the gallant English underdog, is not shown to commit any brutality. But the creative engagement with the Souldan's downfall ends up speaking about what has been silenced. The actions of the English hero produce terrible destruction. The great man has bloody hands.

The text's ambivalence is not a symptom of Spenser's closet liberalism. He endeavours to reproduce the imagery of English heroism, but the contradictions of the whole colonial project make difficulties. We can see some of the knots in A *View*. He moves from a description of the famine following wars in Munster to an attempt to explain the role of the queen and the 'slandering' of Lord Grey. Already he has both constructed and then unsuccessfully devalued a harrowing picture of famine victims by claiming the Irish brought it on themselves. Then he continues:

> if it shall happen that the state of this misery and lamentable image of things shall be told and feelingly presented to her sacred majesty—being by nature full of mercy and clemency, who is most inclinable to such pitiful complaints and will not endure to hear such tragedies made of her people and poor subjects as some about her may insinuate—then she perhaps for very compassion of such calamities will not only stop the stream of such violence and return to her wonted mildness, but also con them little thanks which have been the authors and counsellors of such bloody platforms. So ... Lord Grey, when ... he had brought things almost to this pass ... that it was even made ready for reformation and might have been brought to what her majesty would, like complaint was made against him: that he was a bloody man and regarded not the life of her subjects no more than dogs ... Ear was soon lent thereunto; all suddenly turned topsydeturvy. He noble lord eftsoons was blamed
>
> (pp. 159–60)

The passage has to maintain an image of Elizabeth's clemency, even while Spenser is aware that some doubt this. He has to focus on her personal disposition, her 'nature', and distance this from the structure of her rule. Hence he needs to refer to the doubters; but in doing so, admits their existence and thus produces doubt in the reader. The same strategy, and difficulties, may be seen in the description of

Mercilla. She is a clear image for Elizabeth, and is used to 'explain' Elizabeth's merciful attitude to Mary Queen of Scots ... which culminated in Mary's execution. Thus Mercilla is presented as personally tender, by nature. But one of the first sights in her court is that of a poet with his tongue nailed to a post. On a notice over his head is written

> In cyphers strange, that few could rightly read,
> BON FONT: but bon that once had written bin,
> Was raced out, and Mal was now put in.
> So now Malfont was plainely to be red;
> (5.9.26)

The hand that changed the notice is unknown and invisible; the sentence of torture is passed by an unidentified power. Spenser's choice of tense enables him, crucially, not to name the subject of the verb. The creator of texts is victim of a hand that can alter texts. The judgement is plain, but a *few* people can still read the word Bon under Mal. To those people, and the poem's reader, the arbitrary justice has produced a text which is unstable in that it always reveals two opposed meanings, always exhibits both the doubt and the arbitrariness of its own judgement.

The particular difficulty in the passage from A *View* occurs, then, around Lord Grey. He had almost done what the queen wanted when he was slandered. So the queen's natural pity, as a person, turns her against Grey. But this means she has been duped, by false slanders. Here's the trap. If she was to be seen as not duped, then her motive may not have been pity. And anyway, where did Grey get his idea that he was doing what the queen wanted? Unspoken, but causing all the trouble, is Spenser's knowledge that the state required brutality, that colonialism suppresses before it 'civilises'. And the queen had supported Grey's massacre of the Spaniards at Smerwick. The tension between the political realities and the official imagery cannot be concealed. Spenser could produce official imagery, but he could not gloss over contradictions which shaped his own social circumstances. His text here attempts to sort out apparent inconsistencies in the state he served. The queen needed to slap down Grey, precisely because he had been so successful. But for Spenser Grey's success had promised employment and security. In devaluing Grey's policies the queen produced dangers for those who served her, yet she simultaneously was the guarantor of future service. Spenser's texts, however unwittingly, engage modern readers within the contradictions that go to the heart of the Renaissance regime.

I want to finish this chapter by returning to the text which most students of Spenser have to read, and which I may be accused of substantially avoiding in order to make many of my previous points. My example from it is intended to show how contradiction shapes the episode, in its language and argument, and also to look at a subject hitherto ignored but of deep importance: money. In Renaissance England the main source of wealth was land, and if you were born with land you had money. But if you had no landed inheritance, you had to have money in order to purchase land. For the social climber money had a real value, but that value could not be spoken of since for the class he aspired to it was not supposedly the dominant value.

My example is drawn from the famous description of Guyon's visit to Mammon, Book 2, Canto 7. This passage is the subject of numerous commentaries, of which those by Berger (1957) and Quilligan (1983) are useful, and I shall try not to duplicate these. My analysis comes close, however, to Maureen Quilligan's view that Guyon's experiences amount to a 'freelance labourer's critique of late Elizabethan economic realities' (p. 61).

The opening description of Mammon is full of puns. His iron coat is

> A worke of rich entayle, and curious mould,
> Woven with antickes and wild Imagery:
> And in his lap a masse of coyne he told,
> And turned upsidowne, to feede his eye
> And covetous desire with his huge threasury.
>
> (4)

The words describing the coat slip around: it's carved with grotesque designs, but also 'entail' can refer to a legal means of guaranteeing succession of property, 'mould' can mean earth as well as fashioning, 'antickes' also invokes 'antiques', and 'wild' can mean naturally innocent and free as well as licentious and unrestrained. The counting is odd: why does turning the money upside-down feed the desire? Perhaps the consistent image is sexual: the word 'lap' is more specifically genital in Renaissance usage; Mammon's desire comes from seeing the underside of the coin; the hugeness of the treasury in a male lap is an image that's phallic. The puns create an image not entirely pejorative; the sexual image invokes a potency in the 'bad' figure of Mammon. We shall need to return to the instability of this vision.

The money is stamped with images of kings: this is the wealth which takes its value from its circulation in markets and commodity dealing. Guyon says that Mammon's hoarding keeps it from its 'right usaunce'. Mammon speaks of his own power to supply easily the riches and estate 'For which men swinck and sweat incessantly' (8). He then offers wealth to Guyon's 'great mind, or greedy vew' (9). The word-play on great/greedy places Guyon in a world of competition which he himself denies. He says his 'der-doing armes' separate him from weak men who pursue money, and that regard for 'worldly mucke' abases

> the high heroicke spright,
> That joyes for crownes and kingdomes to contend;
> Faire shields, gay steedes, bright armes be my delight:

Those be the riches fit for an advent'rous knight.

(10)

In Guyon an ideal of non-mercenary chivalry is apparently placed against the greed for money. But Guyon's language forgets that the chivalric armaments have to be bought with money, just as in the real world 'der-doing' enterprise, such as Ralegh's, leads to financial gain. What his ideal represses comes up to the surface through a pun, on 'crowns'. This lends a different colour to the activity of contending. Spenser would have known, if Guyon doesn't, that great aristocrats such as Leicester had developed mining projects on their estates and thus produced conditions not dissimilar to those of Mammon's cave into which Guyon descends to encounter the morality of money.

Mammon claims that he can create kings, even from those who lie in the dust. This claim has to be rejected because it runs counter to an idea of inherited and immutable social hierarchy, and to an idea of divine mystique in kingship. Guyon claims that money causes misery, and that it produces civil disorder and ruin in states: 'Castles surprizd, great cities sackt and brent:/So mak'st thou kings, and gaynest wrongfull governement' (13). But Guyon's argument does not destroy Mammon's; his moral argument can coexist with Mammon's economic one, and indeed he ends by conceding that Mammon *can* make kings. Guyon's solution is a personal one: individuals have to control the 'fowle intemperaunce' which leads them to despise their 'native joyes' (15). In recommending his solution Guyon has to appeal to another myth, that we are born with 'native joys' although the world is shaped by Mammon's competition. He goes on to speak of a harmonious golden age, which Mammon then brutally rejects: 'Thou that doest live in later times, must wage/Thy workes for wealth, and life for gold engage' (18). Guyon again retreats to morality: he will not 'receave/Thing offred, till I know it well be got' (19). Thus when Mammon says that his hoard is rightful, Guyon has nothing left to say but to ask to see where it's kept.

In setting Guyon against Mammon Spenser's text produces a critique of both systems of values. What is at stake is not moral principle but social organisation. Guyon says that he chooses to spend his time in arms and 'to be Lord of those, that riches have,/Then them to have my selfe, and be their servile sclave' (33). This choice envisages a sort of feudal relationship that guarantees the lord's innocence from wealth-producers, and that prefers personal rule and loyalties to a system of mercantile relations. Guyon later adds that he doesn't need more money and asks to be free 'to follow mine emprise' (39). Guyon's position sustains the idea that enterprise can be dissociated from a world which competes over wealth. The key notion is 'free': Spenser's heroes seek to be free to act, to conquer, to avoid contradictions. When Philip Sidney told the queen that 'the difference of degrees between free men, could not challenge any other homage than precedency' (in Montrose, 1977, p. 23) he was arguing, as a gentleman, against the feudal power of great lords. He wanted to be free to compete for wealth and preferment without the shackles of feudal structure. In establishing a bond of personal merit and loyalty to the queen he was asking for her support as absolute and 'personal' ruler against the great lords; so too Spenser's heroes overthrow all sorts of established rulers in the course of their personal service to Gloriana.

Guyon's chivalric idealism is a legend of feudal society that Spenser knew to be decaying; it can never destroy the money economy of Mammon, that Spenser knew to be all too real. This is perhaps why the first picture of Mammon is both so unstable and so potent. Yet Mammon's ideas of continual competition threaten the security of the landed estate that Spenser was using his money to obtain, and are thus intolerable. Spenser puts the ideas into his text in order to put them down. But the effort of doing this in turn leads into a tangle. The text is caught where Spenser found himself, between a collapsing feudalism and an emerging wealth-producing order (though the text, in its necessary devaluing of Mammon, can't admit that he produces anything). The solution to the contradiction is to admit that one *is* implicated in the money world, but to insist on behaving virtuously in it. This is where the whole idea of individual morality becomes necessary to Spenser's outlook. It solves in fiction the problems which emerge from the all too real economic issues.

I have deliberately introduced ideas of personal morality at the end of an argument about social issues, because the two are connected. It is possible to lose sight of their connection, both in the texts of Spenser and in those of the moralistic commentators. The connection between the two is to be relevant to the next chapter.

# 2

# Sex

## A. *Scudamour at the Temple of Venus*

No book of literary criticism can any longer ignore sexual
politics. For the greater part of this century women and
homosexuals have been battling against oppression and
exploitation. The fight was waged in the streets, the
workplaces, and some sections of the 'academy'. It has now
become respectable for many male academics to recognise
feminism, though that recognition is still only rarely
accompanied by political activities other than writing; and
gay politics remains not just unrespectable but in many
forms illegal. A 'new reading' of any author must attend to
sex and sexuality, not simply because these are trendy topics,
but because we have learnt that they are part of the
organisation of society and the definition of the individual.

The following analysis of Spenser begins with the links
between sex and economics. I make this emphasis because
'man' and 'woman' are not unchanging categories that exist
outside society and history. The biology may remain the

same, but ideas of social role and definitions of sexual identity change within different social formations. My critical method has tended to follow that of Anglo-American feminist criticism, which concentrates on how women are portrayed within narratives—what qualities, role, characteristics are attributed to them. More recent, continentally influenced, feminist criticism looks at how texts are put together as well as what is portrayed in them, and tries to identify masculine language, masculine narrative, etc. While I have attempted to identify the 'male gaze', most of this latter work on Spenser still remains to be done.

My starting-point is Scudamour's narrative of his visit to the Temple of Venus (*Faerie Queene* 4.10). The squire of low birth tells first how he intends to 'purchase' a place among the best:

> this same brave emprize for me did rest,
> And that both shield and she whom I behold,
> Might be my lucky lot; sith all by lot we hold.
>
> (4)

The journey to Venus's Temple is masculine enterprise to achieve 'shield' and 'she' (alliteratively balanced). This enterprise allows entry to an elite, a 'place' marked by achievement of the coat of arms (and the woman comes as a free bonus with it: stanza 8). Scudamour's use of the word 'lot' shifts in meaning, between the *winnable* and the *destined*. This shift indicates the social reality behind his fantasy. In feudal society great aristocrats owned land and place by inheritance, but enterprise, particularly in the colonies, could nevertheless make its own gains—even if these were seen as less respectable. The Temple is here defended by a castle with knights who 'maintaine that castels ancient rights' (7): the adventurer specifically has to combat 'ancient rights'. Scudamour confronts Doubt, and Delay who threatens 'time to steale, the threasure of mans day,/Whose smallest minute lost no riches render may' (14). Again, it is the entrepreneur, rather than the feudal lord, who needs to turn time into money. Thus the narrative has the reader side with the adventurer and his goals.

In introducing the 'reader', I want to recall a point I made earlier which has specific bearing on the analysis of sex and sexuality. Irrespective of Spenser's dedication to the queen as supreme reader, the text of *The Faerie Queene* assumes a male readership, in that it offers points of identification available to men only and objects of desire culturally designated for men rather than women (I should add here that I am grateful to Elaine Hobby, of Loughborough University, for compelling me to take account of the different position of the woman reader; my first draft had shared Spenser's blindness to this issue). In terms of pleasure and identification there is little point of entry for the woman reader. In modern society most of those who read *The Faerie Queene* are students: since the majority of students of English literature are women, this point about their exclusion from the text has become crucial. Within the power-relations of the academy, women students are offered a male-authored poem by male or (often) male-identified teachers which they are expected to find important and beautiful yet which offers them little point of entry. The result is not simply alienation from one text, but a sense of exclusion from a structure of learning and validation.

This general issue may be seen to have particular application to the narrative I am concerned with here. Some critics suggest that Scudamour's adventure is treated ironically, and that far from being one of the poem's heroes his attitudes and moral status create problems for Amoret (and he can't get through the flames to rescue her from the House of Busirane, though Britomart can). Although I would not dispute these general observations about

Scudamour, I would expect to find some signals in this section of narrative that indicate irony or disapproval (I concede that it is part of Spenser's technique to seduce the reader into false positions, but usually there are sufficient signs to keep alert the 'godly' or scholarly reader). While our attention is directed to Scudamour's misery and 'overboldness' as his story begins, once that story is underway his boldness is revalued as a useful quality against various enemies and temptations; and furthermore, the more his boldness leads him on, the more sights he and we see, the more narrative excitement there is. The central pleasure here, I'd suggest, derives, as in so much of the rest of the poem, from the thrill of male questing, and as such it escapes ironisation. Spenser, always alert to the barbarity of heroes, may attempt, locally, a critique of Scudamour, but the greater part of his text produces a straightforward pleasure in Scudamour's adventure.

The effort to read this passage as irony is itself interesting. It comes, I think, from an anxiety about ensuring that the great author (Spenser) is acceptable to modern society (this role of tidying up authors for every new generation is the service historically performed by the academic servants of 'great Literature'). So there are attempts to locate 'feminist' thought in Spenser, to celebrate his 'strong' heroines and his send-ups of masculinity. The concept of feminism being used here seems to be very vague (that is, as seen by a male outsider: I am an anti-heterosexist, anti-patriarchal man, who has worked in close and creative political alliances with feminists, but I am not a woman). The problem about the sort of feminism being practised in the academy is one for women, both in and outside the academy, to fight over; my only contribution here is to suggest that 'feminism' is not a transhistorical concept and, if there is any pro-woman position in Spenser's writing, then it will be constructed in Renaissance terms, within Renaissance ideology and seeking to engage with the specifics of real Renaissance life. We need to get that right first. An improperly conceptualised 'Spenserian feminism' will not offer women students any real point of entry, because it will itself be something fake.

The sexually radical reading of Spenser may need to be prepared to face the fact, eventually, that there is nothing 'feminist' about his work. But it has a second task, which is to engage with the sexism of so much of the commentary on Spenser. I shall be citing some specific examples later. What concerns us here, however, is a section of the Scudamour narrative and the reader's response. This response is frequently directed by editorial apparatus.

In A. C. Hamilton's edition the notes attempt to stress a critique of Scudamour, often by citing textual parallels, although these may have much less effect on the reader than the present pleasures of the narrative. The editing tidies up Spenser's handling of Scudamour. This is in line with other moments: for example a note on Book 5. 6.3 says 'Artegall's constancy and Britomart's lack of faith illustrate the Homily "Of the state of matrimonie": "For the woman is a weak creature ..."', yet the text has earlier told us that Artegall was 'justly damned by the doome/Of his owne mouth' (5. 5. 17); his 'constancy' is more problematic than the editor wants. While the men are tidied up, the women are circumscribed by a 'correct' idea of femininity. In his introduction to Book 3, specifically the Busirane episode, Hamilton refers us to his opinion 'that Amoret was bound by womanly [!] fears of masculine "maisterie".... . Fowler (1970) 47–58 argues that Amoret fears the physical surrender of marriage, specifically sexual penetration' (p. 303). The editing of that passage notes phallic symbols and speaks of sexual fears; when Spenser's text asks 'who can love the worker of her smart?', Hamilton quotes another poem: 'ye faire Nimphs, which oftentimes have loved/ The cruell worker of your kindly smarts' (p. 418), and in doing so contradicts Spenser's point here.

The editing is interested in promoting an ('erotic') image of femininity terrified by masculine sexuality; it even manages to make the woman knight Britomart more conventionally 'feminine'. It is in the context of these larger assumptions about gender that we have to see the particular promotion of an ironic reading of Scudamour. The male-authored poem is serviced by a male editor for a male readership. It is significant that Hamilton says: 'For any reader the Garden of Adonis episode is a mysterious, but central and initiatory moment to his possessing the whole poem' (p. 302)—'any' ... 'his'? It's not just a male reader, but one who want to 'possess' the poem. That possession is made easier if the poem can be tidied up so that it reinforces the reader's ideas about sexuality and gender. With all these cautions in mind, we now may return to the specific case in hand.

The social and moral significance of enterprise are clarified when Scudamour confronts Danger. Although one of the 'meanest' by birth, Scudamour is not one of those who 'Either through gifts, or guile, or such like waies,/ Crept in by stouping low, or stealing of the kaies' (18): he assaults Danger with 'manhood stout'. Masculinity is defined as the legitimate behaviour by which mean men get rewards. The entrepreneur is worthy of 'grace'. The word 'grace' is both frequent and various in The Faerie Queene. Scudamour had earlier used it to denote a form of stoicism (2) which empowers the individual, against 'common sence', to remain 'settled' in the face of cares. Elsewhere it is associated with a woman's favour to a man, monarch's to a knight, God's to humanity. It is never fixed to one meaning, because its main function is to give the blessing to (or to make ideologically legitimate, good, normal) a variety of different sorts of individual enterprise. Scudamour can earn grace, riches and woman despite his mean birth by exercising his 'manhood'.

This progress sidesteps the debate around 'nurture' (social training) and 'nature' (instinctive ability), which the poem never resolves. 'Manhood' is something the individual is born with, irrespective of rank, but its proper functioning depends on the individual's self-discipline and morality. The exercise of it makes gains, and these are legitimate because manhood is moral.

Once through the obstacles Scudamour has a vision of the paradise within. Art and nature combine to produce sensual pleasure. The vision of 'plenty' is conceived as wealth 'enricht with natures threasure'. But Scudamour's delight is not in fact disconnected from the world of competition. He says that souls in the 'Elysian fields', if they could see this paradise, 'soone would loath their lesser happinesse' and would want to return to life 'That in this joyous place they mote have joyance free' (23). As so often in Spenser's work, moments of bliss or pleasure are described in terms of competition or division. This paradise, better than Elysian fields, will produce envy in the souls and a desire for an impossible resurrection. Thus the vision of sensual pleasure is simultaneously a continual frustration. It is not an alternative to a competitive world but an extension of it. Souls can be 'free' in this place. This again is a crucial word, denoting generosity, liberty, control over one's life. Its significance appears in a sonnet Spenser wrote to his great friend Gabriel Harvey, who fears not the world but 'freely doest of what thee list entreat,/ Like a great lord of peerelesse liberty': the pun on 'peerelesse' shows that the desired freedom relates not just to individual morality but to one's place in class-structured society. To act as free individual is to challenge the authority of peers. To get to his paradise, Scudamour goes through obstacles. It is 'free', to the victor. But it is not an equality for all. The paradise is 'disloignd from common gaze' (24). The text relates this pleasure to individual achievement; part of the pleasure consists in remembering those who can't have what the victor sees.

Scudamour sees lovers who 'by themselves did sport':

> But farre away from these, another sort
> Of lovers lincked in true harts consent;
> Which loved not as these, for like intent,
> But on chast vertue grounded their desire,
> Farre from all fraud, or fayned blandishment; (26)

The next stanza makes plain that this other 'sort' are male 'friends' or homosexual lovers. The text stresses that these lovers are 'chast' and do not love 'for like intent'; they are given a privileged place in paradise but the activity of physical sex is denied. Such denial is in keeping with widespread Renaissance strictures against sodomy, but it also relates specifically, as we shall see, to Spenser's horrified fascination with male sexuality. (The 'hindparts' of Danger are the most 'deformed fearefull ugly' part of him.)

The vision of these lovers has a significant effect on Scudamour:

> I thought there was none other heaven then this;
> And gan their endlesse happinesse envye,
> That being free from feare and gealosye,
> Might frankely there their loves desire possesse;
> Whilest I through paines and perlous jeopardie,
> Was forst to seeke my lifes deare patronesse: (28)

He envies the lovers' escape from a world of competition (fear and jealousy). They are in full and free (frank) *possession* of their desire (contrasting oddly with the claimed chastity). He can never attain this state, since for him the real world is that of quest. He learns to value his individual struggle to gain a woman who is both sponsor and prize: her value to him increases because of *his* effort. The world of the heterosexual quest is competitive and separate from the world of idealised male-bondings.

I stress the value of this ideal masculine world because Spenser himself has already stressed it. In Canto 8 he explains why Arthur, Aemilia and Amoret accept the hospitality of Sclaunder:

> that age despysed nicenesse vaine,
> Enur'd to hardnesse and to homely fare,
> Which them to warlike discipline did trayne,
> And manly limbs endur'd with litle care
> Against all hard mishaps and fortunelesse misfare.
>
> (27)

Just as Scudamour's manhood is opposed to cowardly ambition, so the 'age' of Arthur is opposed to an implicitly modern 'niceness'. Ancient toughness and simplicity are qualities admired from *The Shepheardes Calender* onwards. The 'antique age' lived 'like an innocent,/ In simple truth and blamelesse chastitie'; when 'each unto his lust did make a lawe,/ From all forbidden things his liking to withdraw' (30). This age is free of disordering competition. Furthermore, although Spenser is narrating about Arthur and two women, he speaks only of 'manly limbs'. The self-policing chaste antique world is innocent and male. The modern world, and the difficult adventures of *The Faerie Queene* in general, are marked by competition over female sex objects and by destruction initiated by female sexual evil. (The stress on a male bonding under threat from female sex objects is not necessarily Spenser's invention. Versions of it can be found in medieval poetry: *Gawain and the Green Knight*, Chaucer's *Knight's Tale*. We very much need to chart and explain the currency of these sorts of narratives and imagery. The virile host to whom Gawain passes on kisses is also the Green Knight whose axe calculatedly nicks Gawain's neck, all within a problematising of feudal loyalties and knightly heroism. The emphasis is different in Spenser, for whom there is more positive value attached to the knightly bonding, an innocence that *Gawain* disallows; but nevertheless, insofar as he knew of these stories, they presumably confirmed his ideological concept of 'antiquity'.)

Spenser's ideal vision contains difficulties. When he speaks of 'forbidden things' in the antique age, he omits to explain what they are, why they are forbidden and who has done the forbidding. The general 'blameless chastity' is founded on 'lust' controlled by personal law. Such a problematic ideal has to be carefully positioned within Scudamour's narrative. Scudamour says 'I, that never tasted blis' while he gazes at the paradisal vision. The 'I' here is defined as a person desiring bliss and fulfilment, and the text pauses to gratify this desire by describing, and therefore in a sense providing, for the reader (and viewer) something which it claims cannot be possessed. The next stanza speedily redefines the 'I' as a questor: 'Yet all those sights, and all that else I saw,/ Might not my steps withhold' (4.10.29). And the pleasurable ideal vision, over which the text pauses, is dismissed as nothing more than a delay. In speaking of the 'personal' and sexual, Spenser like so many people reveals his deepest ideological concerns. The ideal vision breaks into the narrative, only to be apologised for and terminated.

My digression from the sequence of Scudamour's narrative was intended to stress Spenser's ideological versions of economic enterprise and sexual competition. The two are closely related, one often working as metaphor for the other. Now we return to Scudamour in the inner temple, where he sees the figure of Venus standing on an altar of 'some costly masse' (Spenser's descriptions are ever alert to the cost of things). Venus is covered in a veil to conceal from people's knowledge that she has double sex. She can beget and conceive in one person, but it is in no way a sexual threat. By contrast, around Venus are damsels, of whom the first is 'Womanhood':

> that she exprest
> By her sad semblant and demeanure wyse:
> For stedfast still her eyes did fixed rest,
> Ne rov'd at random after gazers guyse,
> Whose luring baytes oftimes doe heedlesse harts entyse.
>
> (49)

Woman is ideally defined as serious and wise, accompanied by, in *this* order, shamefastness, cheerfulness, modesty, courtesy, silence, obedience. These qualities contrast with those of the questor. It is stressed that the eyes of the ideal woman do not rove at random; but there is always, however, the potential to entice. Whereas Venus with her male capacity to beget is no threat, the possibility of active female sexual desire ('luring') is one. Woman is to be gazed at; Scudamour does the gazing, and the (male) reader is encouraged to do likewise.

Scudamour then sees Amoret, and debates what to do:

> For sacrilege me seem'd the Church to rob,
> And folly seem'd to leave the thing undonne,
> Which with so strong attempt I had begonne.
> Tho shaking off all doubt and shamefast feare,
> Which Ladies love I heard had never wonne
> Mongst men of worth, I to her stepped neare,
> And by the lilly hand her labour'd up to reare.
>
> (53)

His 'strong attempt' will not be overmastered by religious awe. He justifies himself ideologically by appeal to a notion of 'men of worth'. Specifically he shakes off what accompanies women, 'shamefast' fear. The customary alliteration is organised in the last line not just to recall the Orpheus story but to balance 'lilly' against 'labour'd', thereby defining him as active worker against her as delicate picture. When he is reproached by Womanhood, he quells her into terror by displaying his shield. For on the shield is a

picture of Cupid with 'killing bow/ And cruell shafts'.
Cupid's phallic weaponry is used by the questing male
precisely to terrify the virginal woman. 'For no intreatie',
says Scudamour, would he forego 'so glorious spoyle' (55).
The dominant image is of adventurer as looter, uncon-
strained by decorum. He leads the weeping Amoret away.
She cannot 'her wished freedome fro me wooe' (57). The
quest ends with the capture of a woman, despite her own
wishes.

## B. Elizabeth's 'Arse-kissing Poet'

This reading of Scudamour's narrative may now be
extended to other texts. Some idea of the ideological
importance of a primitive innocent world of male bonding
may clarify the opening of The Shepheardes Calender. In
'Januarye' Colin complains of love melancholy but explains

> It is not Hobbinol, wherefore I plaine,
> Albee my love he seeke with dayly suit:
> His clownish gifts and curtsies I disdaine,
> (55-57)

Colin in fact loves Rosalind, who in turn scorns him. The
unrequited love causes Colin to disregard his flock and break
his pipe. The triangular relationship, in which Colin is both
desired and desirer, is returned to. Halfway through, in
'June', Colin and Hobbinol speak of Colin's melancholy and
poetic skills. The direction of the desire remains uncertain.
Colin tells Hobbinol: 'I blesse thy state,/ That Paradise has
found, whych Adam lost'; Hobbinol joins Colin in blaming
'faithlesse Rosalind' 'That art the roote of all this ruthfull
woe' (9-10, 115-16). The play on 'roote' 'ruthfull' calls
attention to the clever text, away from the imagined

67

Rosalind. In the final eclogue, in the stanza which EK tells us is a summary of the whole work, the last two lines stress the centrality of Hobbinol within the Colin–Rosalind relationship: 'Adieu good Hobbinol, that was so true,/ Tell Rosalind, her Colin bids her adieu' (155–56). While the distress over a woman undoes the poet's skills, the other man has the job of bearing the poet's messages and texts. In 'Aprill' it is of course Hobbinol that sings Colin's hymn to Eliza. The hymn with its official heterosexual courtly language is prefaced, perhaps antagonistically, by allusion to the frustrated 'private' love of males.

It is clear from EK's notes to 'Januarye' that homosexual desire is being spoken of: 'In thys place seemeth to be some savour of disorderly love, which the learned call paederastice: but it is gathered beside his meaning'. Despite the disclaimer, he gives a Platonic definition to 'paederastice' as a love of souls and 'so is paederastice much to be praeferred before gynerastice, that is the love whiche enflameth men with lust toward woman kind'. He hastily forbids anyone to think that he defends 'execrable and horrible sinnes of forbidden and unlawful fleshlinesse' (pp. 422–23). This repeats the strategy in Scudamour's narrative, where physical homosex was denied while homoerotic bondings were suggested. Needless to say, EK's lead has been followed by modern commentators (except Berger, 1983). They ignore homosexuality or see it as abnormal: 'The desperate struggle of womanhood (Amoret) to remain true to normal physical love (Scudamour) despite the attraction of a latent Lesbianism or homosexuality (Busyrane) would account for Amoret's intense suffering' (Hankins, 1971, p. 163). It is difficult to see how, since Busyrane is male, his threat to Amoret is lesbian. More interesting is the notion of a womanhood which is always potentially lesbian (and not of course a manhood which is always potentially homosexual): the illogic here suggests that the roots of the analysis are deep

in the interests of the commentator. The author of Coles
*Notes* plays safe by asserting, completely against Spenser's
own stress, that the 'noblest type of love' is 'love in marriage'
(p. 83). The critical industry busies itself as earnestly with
making a proper heterosexual Spenser as it does with making
a 'sage and serious' one. Alpers (1967) tells us that 'Spenser
is interested not in a character, but in the beautiful maiden
who arouses erotic desire and is constantly being pursued'.
This rape fantasy (in which the maiden is not a 'character'),
far from being condemned, is to be commended since it
'stimulates some of his most interesting poetry about human
desire' (p. 194). Needless to say, the reader about whose
sensitivity Alpers is so concerned is always a heterosexual
male. Tonkin (1973) says that Britomart's 'tears and
tantrums' are a 'womanish reaction ... precipitated by an
unreasoning yet psychologically valid longing for hearth and
home and femininity'. This sounds oddly reminiscent of a
famous Nazi slogan. As an expert on women Tonkin says of
Mirabella: 'This is good psychology: a heartless woman
pours scorn upon her lover most abundantly when she has
an audience, preferably male' (1972, p. 91). Presumably he
knows. Berger (1957) asks of Belphoebe, 'Why does she
dress and grace herself? An answer quickly arises: Belphoebe
is a woman'; we have already learnt that 'she shares the love
of finery characteristic of more human women'. Which all
goes to show that Spenser understood girls, even modern
ones.

The effect of this critical writing is to invite us to see these
women as sex objects, and thus in a sense to 'normalise' the
sexual interests of Spenser's texts (of course for the woman
reader the invitation to see fictional women as sex objects is
far from being an unproblematic or even acceptable
'normality'). By contrast it is worth recalling the relationship
created in the published correspondence between Spenser
and his friend Gabriel Harvey (Hobbinol). In one letter we

have a picture of the two men in bed translating verses; but, they say, that was usual for Renaissance chappies. (By the way, Harvey's homosexuality can be mentioned by critics: he is less famous.) More revealing is the jokiness about Spenser's wife or woman associate at this time: she is not described as a real person, but is given mock names in Latin prose. One section (in Latin) has her wondering why Harvey has not responded to her letters; Harvey in turn calls her 'bellissima Collina Clouta', thus making her into an extension of Spenser's fiction. I may be wrong, but this looks like more than the woman as usual not getting a look in: 'she' seems to be only a game between two male writers, who speak of her in the very language which she, in an unequal education system, may not have understood. In Spenser's work, as in that of so many of his contemporaries, the woman is valued to the extent to which she is appreciated by other men. For example in many sonnet sequences the male poet speaks to a male reader about a desired woman: the male–female relationship might be the one on display, but the male–male relationship is the one being constructed by the text. Spenser tells the story of Mirabella who is beautiful but scornful; she did not realise that

> beautie is more glorious bright and clere,
> The more it is admir'd of many a wight,
> And noblest she, that served is of noblest knight.
>
> (6.7.29)

A woman's beauty depends on the appreciators not the person herself; she is noble insofar as she is served by a noble man. Woman has no autonomous value; her value is derived from the world of men in which, like a coin, she circulates (see Montrose, 1983). Hobbinol sings Colin's hymn to Eliza as a compliment to Colin.

Relations with the woman eventually lead back to

appreciation of the man. For example, Arthur and Artegall battle with each other in a development of a conflict which began with their efforts to save a woman from two 'pagan' knights. The woman points out the pagans are dead and appeals to them to stop, offering herself as a target for their fury. They open their helmets:

> Tho when as Artegall did Arthure vew,
> So faire a creature, and so wondrous bold,
> He much admired both his heart *and hew*,
> And touched with intire affection, nigh him drew.
> (5.8.12; my italic)

The narrative now excludes the woman as the knights draw together. Arthur is the visual centre. She only has her plight inquired into *after* the men have sworn loyalty to each other. Such loyalty-swearing is taken to be a harmless feature of late feudal or Renaissance society, with its cultural stress on codes of friendship between men. These codes certainly played their part in ideologically organising a society in which the transmission of power was both male and personal. While feminism has as it were penetrated the academy sufficiently for critics to accept that the friendship code excludes women, there is still, however, a difficulty about accepting the potentially sexual charge within Renaissance friendship. Yet much of the newest research, principally undertaken by gay academics, is showing that the use of, and associations with, the concept of friendship indicate a clear sexual dimension, albeit coded as a result of social taboos (for Ben Jonson, in *Bartholomew Fair*, a classic friendship story is an obvious target for sodomitical jokes). It is in the light of this research that I insist on the homoerotic potentiality in Spenser's work.

Let's move, therefore, to a more explicitly sexual example, that of Amyas and Poeana: a squire of low birth is loved, and kept prisoner, by the daughter of a giant. He remains loyal to his lady, Aemylia, while Poeana allows him some freedoms in exchange for sex. He is helped by his friend Placidas who not only looks like him but can reciprocate Poeana's embraces since he has no former commitment. Placidas explains that he tricked Poeana 'To my friends good, more then for mine owne sake,/ For whose sole libertie I love and life did stake' (4.8.60). While having the sex intended for Amyas, Placidas thinks not of himself but of his friend's advantage. The lust of the enemy woman leads to a more intimate realisation of the male bond. When Placidas gets out, he is greeted by Amyas's lover

> mindlesse of her wonted modestie,
> She to him ran, and him with streight embras
> Enfolding said, And lives yet Amyas?
>
> (63)

The embrace a modest woman only normally gives to her lover is here given to the absent lover's friend. Placidas is the medium through which female desire and concern for Amyas passes. He is the one who knows if Amyas lives. The male bonding in this story is the primary unit. We have been told already: 'Aemylia well he lov'd, as I mote ghesse;/ Yet greater love to me then her he did professe' (57).

The Amyas story is an appropriate example for the Book of Friendship. At the start of the next canto, before the story continues, Spenser shows he already has a model of sorts of love into which the friendship fits:

> The deare affection unto kindred sweet,
> Or raging fire of love to woman kind,
> Or zeale of friends combynd with vertues meet.

These are not all equal:

But of them all the band of vertuous mind
Me seemes the gentle hart should most assured bind.

(9.1)

The theoretical formulation insists on abstract 'virtue', whereas the story itself hinged on the physicality, and explicitly sexual substitutions, of the two men. This real interest of the narrative is ignored by the poem's own commentary. The elevation of male-bonding over hetero-sexual partnership is justified as appropriate to 'gentle hart'. That adjective houses a tension between specific class connotation and a more 'personal' meaning. In a society where power and wealth were based on personal inheritance and kinship, marriage was a means of consolidating estates and property rights. The woman of a gentry family was used as the device for linking the power-holding males of both her own and another family. In a social structure consolidated by arranged and property-based marriages the woman is valued only insofar as she is exchangeable between male-run groups. Spenser's romance stories of lovers and friends may end with women saved and lovers united, but they also show the power and primacy of the male-bond. The mutual male appreciation is expressed in personal (though not sexual) terms; as such, it is a romance version of mutual economic appraisal. Yet the narrative's interest in the personal prowess of men also performs another function, in that it sees heroes as those who triumph through individual accomplishment rather than through their inherited status. The text may be said to eroticise competitive individualism in that it fantasises the power of the freely acting male and also desires to join a group of mutually appreciating males. In *economic* terms there's a contradiction between competition and stability, but as *erotic* fantasy it can remain coherent.

These points about men have been made by attending to the shifts, ambiguities and, perhaps, 'unconscious' elements of the narration. By contrast, in the presentation of women Spenser's text is not so much ambiguous as repetitive. Women are shown as disrupters of male community: Duessa's beauty is a scheme to distract Redcross from his quest; the false Florimell is invented to produce bloody rivalry between knights; revelation of Radigund's beauty leads to Artegall's imprisonment and loss of masculine identity. That men show weakness in falling for women only confirms how necessary it is to resist female conspiracy. Lust is said to produce blindness to the worth of virtuous friendship.

The pattern of female effects on men may be verified in most of the stories. The next step is to ask why *The Faerie Queene* is so full of such stories. In answering this question I am drawing on critical theories that interest themselves in the place of ideologies in the fictional text, and in the text's role in reproducing ideology. Such theories argue that the author's mind, like all of ours, is shaped by and to some extent critical of the dominant ideologies in society. Thus the artwork shows both conscious attempts to reproduce or question ideas and 'unconscious' failures to think through, to face a contradiction, to challenge an idea which feels natural, good or right. It is possible to explain why an author has found pleasing a particular story, or why she or he has imagined a particular fiction. Fictions don't pop out of nowhere but are born in ideology.

I have argued that Spenser has a fictional ideal of a male world without strife. By contrast the real world he knew was one in which competition between powerful men undermined projects of social and financial construction. This specifically applied to Spenser's experience of Ireland. My analysis of *A View* argued that the debilitating competition grew out of the very process of consolidation, and was hence an inescapable contradiction. But in the work on his poetic project, Spenser's imagination is permitted to produce a fiction which is satisfying because it offers an apparent way out of the contradiction. This fiction is also satisfying because it stays within the safety of certain traditional ideas. It suggests that men compete because they are blinded by lust. Dominant ideology in the Renaissance associated lust with passion, riot, disorder, chaos. Thus a perceived disorder that has its real roots in economic competition can now be explained, in fiction, as a failure of reason induced by passion, which is in turn induced by lust for women.

The fiction performs an ideological reversal: the disorder which originated within male society is explained as a threat to it from outside. For what could be more outside men than women? A specific example may illustrate the general principle. In the description of the tournament for false Florimell appears one of those unstable similes. The two virtuous friends Cambell and Triamond fight the other knights:

> As when two greedy wolves doe breake by force
> Into an heard, farre from the husband farme,
> They spoile and ravine without all remorse,
> So did these two through all the field their foes enforce.
>
> (4.4.35)

Their 'bolde emprize' is imaged as wolves destroying a flock: enterprise goes with destruction, great men are barbarians. But here another explanation is available, provided by the fiction which dreamt up the tournament. Remember the knights battle for false Florimell: their aggression may thus be attributed to the malign influence of an evil woman. The endemic moral instability of heroes can be transformed into a woman-derived affliction.

My remarks about the portrayal of women and men, and about Spenser's 'necessary' fictions, are leading up to an analysis of Britomart. This figure has received much critical attention and may be superficially explained as a borrowing from the Italian epic poet Ariosto (though we must still ask why Ariosto's Bradamante appealed to Spenser) or as a poetic image of Elizabeth I. The imagery that surrounded and reproduced the power of the monarch has received extensive modern analysis, which has shown how the language about sex and desire is a political language. It is now generally accepted that the imagery of lovers' service to a monarch who is both virgin and mother is a figurative expression of the power relations of monarch, courtiers and noble rivals. This work on love language and Elizabeth's imagery has tended, however, to play down the other aspect of Elizabeth, as 'male-spirited' woman. The focus on (hetero) sexual power-games has obscured the questioning of sexual identity. When Elizabeth's propaganda stressed her 'unwomanly' toughness, it showed she could compete in a male world: that she was a 'phallic woman'. Both aspects matter, in that the tough authority, which many admired, was always potentially in tension with her biological womanhood.

The female knight Britomart wins the tournament for the false Florimell, but refuses the prize since Florimell's beauty 'She lesse esteem'd, then th' others vertuous government' (4.5.20). The girdle fits her protégé Amoret but the male knights, blinded by lust, give it to Florimell. The same resistance to female beauty and insistence on true justice characterise Britomart's suppression of the 'usurped' power of Radigund. She is embarrassed by the humiliated Artegall and reproaches him: 'Where is that dreadfull manly looke?' (5.7.40); she restores male rule in the Amazon city. In her emotions and her public acts Britomart upholds an ideal of proper masculinity. But why must it be a woman who does this? In part because she is a version of Elizabeth: when Britomart fights Artegall the violence has escalated beyond the order of the tournament; this violence is only ended when her face is accidentally revealed, causing Artegall and

Scudamour to fall back in 'obedience' and kneel in worship as if to 'some celestiall vision'. This is like Elizabeth the peace-maker, whose very person supposedly induces a natural and automatic submission (and thus by implication does not need to impose and enforce obedience through state-machinery). (All which amounts to an ideological *mis*representation.)

It is precisely only Britomart's biological womanhood that puts an end to the sequence of increasingly violent masculine competitions. As fictional device she transforms a version of violent society into a desired (but impossible) harmony. Britomart's power derives, however, specifically from *chaste* womanhood. The effect of her 'grave' and 'princely' face on Artegall 'his ranging fancie did refraine,/ And looser thoughts to lawfull bounds withdraw' (4.6.33). Throughout the poem Britomart's chastity produces order and restraint: it is an image of law enforced not by apparatus of state but by the disciplined person of a ruler. This chastity is so useful as a version of political control because it stresses not the forceful imposition of law but the voluntary obedience of the onlooker. It holds out the always possible reward (the beauty) without ever inciting the dangerous competition (lust). It compliments the subject by arousing his virility, yet never permits anarchic desire. It is a restatement of the ideology of absolutism which places power in the person of the monarch. It is pleasurable because it avoids the contradictions of real politics.

But Artegall is special: he is not humiliated by Britomart's gravity, for through restraint 'the passion grew more fierce and faine,/ Like to a stubborne steede whom strong hand would restraine' (33). His masculine power is in fact strengthened. Indeed Britomart herself upholds masculine ideals: she is the armed phallic woman. So in worshipping Britomart, men worship what most preserves themselves. Whereas Acrasia is a threat because she makes men end quests, Britomart sustains questing. In sexual terms, the combination of restraint and increased passion makes sense, whereas in economic or political terms restraint that strengthens an enemy is a contradiction. The sexual narrative does a useful job in making coherent what is contradictory.

Thus far Britomart is working as a version of the Elizabeth myth. The anxiety about biological womanhood returns, however, when Spenser insists on Britomart's specifically female inferiority to the men. Even while the men are in submission, Britomart's old nurse Glauce explains that they had no cause to be jealous that she would woo away their loves 'sith meanes ye see there wants theretoo' (30). Using the nurse in the stereotyped role of comedy—as the sexually knowing companion of innocent girls—the narrative creates innuendo explicitly directed at Britomart's lack of a penis. (In all other ways she had the means to woo ladies away: Amoret is quite attached to her.) Glauce tells Britomart and Artegall that they must behave as lovers and at the end of her speech, 'Thereat full inly blushed Britomart;/ But Artegall close smyling joy'd in secret hart' (32). If Glauce's conclusion that 'lovers heaven must passe by sorrowes hell' is taken as a reference to the 'necessary', and for the woman painful, loss of virginity, then the couple's reactions reproduce supposedly 'normal' gender difference. The woman blushes while the man secretly delights. Later the stereotyping strengthens. Britomart struggles 'with womanish art' to hide signs of her love, and when Artegall has to depart on 'an hard adventure yet in quest' (42) she tries to delay him by fearful talk of the perils. She becomes passive frightened wife; he alone the adventurer.

Britomart like the virgin queen inhibits lust and creates order; but very unlike the queen her biology always makes her eventually inferior to men. (Elizabeth did play the simple maid role, but usually where the very conditions of her performance, for example, a speech to Parliament, insisted simultaneously on her power. Spenser's narrative insists on a more profound vulnerability and implicates the reader in some of the classic sexist ways of looking at women. As I have said I disagree with the view, expressed by Quilligan, that the poem is directed at a female reader.) The female vulnerability of the ruler is exhibited again with Belphoebe: her moralising about courts does not prevent Braggadocchio from attempting rape, an assault from which Belphoebe *flees*. While using her phallic spear Britomart is certainly a supremely successful knight, but disarmed she is a 'normal' and safe woman. As a fiction she unites in one 'character' elements which are, and remain, disparate. She is an ideologically useful creation because she solves the contradictions around masculine aggression without challenging the male claim to rule. Arguably, Spenser's text is interesting for us because its sheer struggle to cope with the various problems ends up revealing (rather than concealing) the ideological tricks. One further point needs making about the woman who upholds masculine ideals. In *A View* Spenser warns against English marrying Irish. He says that marriage to 'vassalls' is a problem in all commonwealths. The reason is that 'the child taketh most of his nature of the mother, besides speech, manners, inclination, which are for the most part agreeable to the conditions of their mothers. For by them they are first framed and fashioned, so as what they received once from them they will hardly ever after forgo' (p. 120). Given the crucial role played by the mother in forming the child, this is the weak point in male-run society since it is a relationship from which men are excluded. Women's influence is always present in the reproduction of a society which attempts to limit women's influence, hence the anxiety about women's role (see Greenblatt, 1980). Particularly vulnerable is the mixed class marriage, where the dominant is always in danger of being undermined by the dominated. Thus the importance of woman showing herself to be the 'equal' of man, and not vice versa.

I have spoken of why female lust and chastity are ideologically 'necessary' to the narratives of *The Faerie Queene*, and I have tried to highlight some of the ideological confusion which makes Spenser's text so revealing. I want to extend this analysis now by looking at descriptions of women, and thus at the role played by a male-authored text in reproducing in a predominantly male readership assumptions about 'woman'.

When Britomart's face is revealed in battle it is 'Deawed with silver drops, through sweating sore,/ But somewhat redder, then beseem'd aright'. Her hair falls loose: 'Like to a golden border did appeare,/ Framed in goldsmithes forge with cunning hand' (4.6.19, 20). Why does this fiction look like this? The blonde hair is not an automatic feature of the beautiful woman (remember the 'dark' mistresses of the 1590s). It's an idealised version of the queen's carrotty curls, and it's carefully Anglo-Saxon. Britomart is a source of light, an alternative to the dark places and wild woods, the areas beyond English rule. The blonde hair is indeed like supreme artifice rather than wildness, and is always dependent on male power—exceeding the skill of the goldsmith but thrown like the sand by the male river, always clean. Part of the beauty is, as Spenser notes, unconventional—the sweat. Belphoebe too praised sweat. It's beautiful because it is a sign of honest work, and because it is the opposite of courtly cosmetics.

Britomart's light is also an alternative to the darkness of wombs and menstrual blood. The flood from Error's 'filthy maw' is part of the poem's recurrent nightmare:

> in the wide wombe of the world there lyes,
> In hatefull darknesse and in deepe horrore,
> An huge eternall Chaos, which supplyes

The substances of natures fruitfull progenyes.
(3.6.36)

Acrasia's pose with Verdant is partly horrifically maternal.
In this context let's place the woundings of Britomart which
frame her adventures in Book 3. Purple blood weeps out and
stains her 'lilly smock'. As Montrose (1983) notes about the
'milk-white' flower of A *Midsummer Night's Dream* that is
stained purple, this could be an image of menstruation. It is
significant, too, that the major distinction between the attire
of Belphoebe and Radigund is that the wicked Amazon wears
a purple rather than 'lylly whight' 'camus'. The purple,
possibly menstrual, blood of Britomart is presented as
weakness, sudden vulnerability, a stain.

The worry, if not horror, about the generative aspects of
women may be explained by reference back to that
quotation from A *View* in which mothers are said to have a
supreme influence on framing children. This power comes
from women's biological status, and it is politically
dangerous because men cannot control it. The existence of
male society literally depended on the biology of women, a
truth which nags away at all Spenser's efforts to shape proper
masculinity. So he has Britomart and Belphoebe discomfited
by their biological womanhood while they praise a model of
work based on masculine enterprise (rather than female
production).

A brief note on Belphoebe might clarify the values of
woman. Her ivory forehead is 'Like a broad table ... For
Love his loftie triumphes to engrave' (2.3.24); her legs are
'Like two faire marble pillours' supporting the temple of the
gods 'Whom all the people decke with girlands greene' (28).
The forehead written over by a male Love, the legs like
decorated pillars: the body is figuratively already written
over. Her breasts 'like young fruit in May/ Now little gan to
swell, and being tide,/ Through her thin weed their places

81

only signifide.' (29) They do not show their shape through her garment, only their 'places'. She has only the biological markings of a woman, but they're barely three-dimensional.

We are told how Belphoebe is to be seen: the colours of her face the 'gazers sense with double pleasure fed' but the eyes 'bereav'd the rash beholders sight' (22,23). Like Britomart she tempers lust in those in the narrative; but nevertheless the poetic description itself provides pleasure for the (male) *reader* (and once again I have to add that I imagine this pleasure becomes much more complex for the heterosexual woman reader; it may be that she sees it as something which is meant to be felt but which is not accessible, and is hence alienating—but who am I to know?). Thus the description of the legs contrives, through the imagery of garlands, to envisage, though half-hid, her pubic hair. There is something legitimately pleasurable because both Belphoebe and Britomart are safe for a masculine world. Belphoebe only has the markings of a woman, Britomart sweats very unlike one. Neither is conceived as a fully sensual, generative, female. That is the condition of their attraction.

The morality of beauty does not remain such a clear-cut issue. When Serena is captured by cannibals, they strip her and gaze at the parts of her body, which are itemised in a list in a manner familiar from courtly poetry (and ironised so well in Sidney's *Astrophel and Stella*). The narrative speaks of the 'sordid eyes' of cannibals, the 'loose lascivious sight' which sees 'daintie parts' 'Which mote not be prophan'd of common eyes' (6.8.41–43). Through the cannibals, who literally want to eat what they slobber over, courtly description is attacked. But even while the text invokes horror at the treatment of Serena, in its itemising stanza it exhibits her body to the reader's interest. The reader imaginatively gazes alongside the 'sordid eyes'.

About the 'gaze': feminist film criticism has identified the notion of the 'male gaze' through analysis of camera movements which construct how the film-viewer sees women in a film-narrative. Such camera work will often show the woman as vulnerable, passive, sexy; as object. (Similarly Renaissance paintings arrange naked female bodies for the consumption of a viewer, though this is non-narrative.) Simply to extend this notion to a non-visual medium such as poetry is difficult, but it's worth noting that the juxtaposition of abstract with descriptive passages highlights what is to be imaginatively looked at. And the use of 'look' and 'sight' words instructs readers to draw upon sights remembered from other artworks or life, and already inevitably imbued with patriarchal values. Literary descriptions of women will often reproduce ideas of what a woman 'is'.

There is much looking in *The Faerie Queene*, often explained in terms of moral structuring. To avoid morality, I shall analyse *Epithalamion*. Spenser writes nominally as himself about his own wife. The poem celebrates her, shows her to us, and presents Spenser's feelings. He uses the familiar catalogue stanza, itemising beautiful bits of her body: this time without attack on courtliness. Before this stanza he refers to her appearance 'like some mayden Queene' (158), but this is not an image of her power. 'Her modest eyes abashed' look at the ground, a sign of submission and vulnerability. She blushes to hear her praises sung by her husband, the poet. He shows her to merchants' daughters, while he employs the usual male poet's device of listed body parts (like a Haynes car manual). The image of the modest maiden queen recalls the 'Aprill' eclogue, another moment of artistic display. The reference here is as much to Spenser's own poetic creations as it is to a real wife. The itemising stanza is, however, followed by reference to her 'heavenly guifts' at which you would stand 'astonisht lyke to those which red/ Medusaes mazeful hed' (189–90).

Medusa's head turns those who look at it to stone; it punishes the improper look. The image is meant to evoke the woman's power over man, but its cultural status as a physical horror (if not an image for female genitalia) undercuts the offered display of her 'inward beauty'. The itemising stanza is framed by two that are alert to the power-relations of looks, but we are not forbidden to see her as ornament. After the wedding, poet and reader look at her while she looks at the ground and 'suffers not one looke to glaunce awry,/ Which may let in a little thought unsownd' (236–37). For her a misplaced glance amounts to moral instability. Her virtue depends on not looking back at us.

When the marriage night approaches the poet asks us to behold how she lies 'In proud humility' (306) like Maia, who was raped by Jove. And although he asks to be covered by night, 'That no man may us see' (320) his images refer us to more of Jove's sex acts (see Greene, 1968). Male sexual activity is kept in focus.

> Ye sonnes of Venus, play your sports at will,
> For greedy pleasure, careless of your toyes,
> Thinks more upon her paradise of joyes,
> Then what ye do, albe it good or ill.
> (364–67)

Poet and reader are, unlike her, aware of the activities of the sons of Venus. Her concentration on her own sexual pleasure makes her morally vulnerable (greedy, careless) to possibly 'ill' actions. This not only puts down her desire, it envisages the male sexual activity as something distanced from her, something good—or ill.

After the sex, women appear in the figures of goddesses, who are asked to make the intercourse fruitful. The poem ends with a compliment to procreation, but specifically the interest is in whether his 'timely seed' will 'informe' the 'chast wombe'. The real woman tends to be forgotten as the poem looks to blessings from heaven. While the sex act stanzas invoked male figures, despite the claim to secrecy, the pregnancy is public, with female figures. These are the terms on which the poem relates to 'woman'. There is little equality of partnership. The final apology for a 'Song made in lieu of many ornaments' (427) looks humble enough, but it is precisely through the 'ornaments' of the poem that the relationship is clarified. The poem is conscious of how women are seen by poetry, but simultaneously uses its own gaze at the woman to control her place in the relationship as it is reproduced in the poem.

The marriage hymn has images of rape; the description of Serena evoked the pleasure it condemned. The texts have a problem with female sexuality. Norbrook (1984) relates Spenser's 'misogyny' to strands in puritan thought. But also woman is the weak point in patriarchy. Furthermore, the sexual effect of woman makes masculine identity unstable.

This last point is forcefully stated in the Bower of Bliss. Guyon resists all until he sees two women wrestling in water. When they see him looking they encourage him further. The display works through revealing and concealing: one shows her 'lilly paps' and everything else that might entice him, 'The rest hid underneath, him more desirous made'. The other lets down her hair

> So that faire spectacle from him was reft,
> Yet that, which reft it, no lesse faire was fownd:
> So hid in lockes and waves from lookers theft,
> Nought but her lovely face she for his looking left.
> (2.12.66, 67)

The scene is not simply about dangerous female beauty, but about how the male gaze is trapped. Guyon's desire is produced by denying him. The wordplay on 'locks' and 'looks', and the double-meaning of 'locks', show how the hair both advertises and locks away the treasure. Sexual flirtation is closely related to problems of possession: it questions what may be seen (stolen/possessed) by the watcher, while it provokes further desire to possess (to see). In its imaginative engagement with these women, Spenser's text is preoccupied as much with economics as with sexuality, for both shape identity. (Greenblatt, 1980, also connects the episode with colonialism, Ireland and religious iconoclasm.)

When Guyon encounters Acrasia and her lover he sees a young man who has abandoned 'advauncement' and spent goods and body in 'wastfull luxuree'. Acrasia's 'snowy brest was bare to readie spoyle/ Of hungry eies, which n'ote therewith be fild'; her eyes 'thrild/ Fraile harts, yet quenched not' (78). She can never be fully possessed. Like silent waves she has dangerous depths beneath a sparkling surface. (Significantly, Guyon is not affected by the maternally posed Acrasia as he is by the wrestling—competing—maidens.) When caught, Acrasia is tied in chains of adamant but her lover is released. This act simplifies the issue of male lust, for it implies that the lover has simply been led astray whereas she is a permanent threat. But while Guyon was watching the wrestlers, the sex desire was produced from within him, by a flirtation that worked on his already existing desire to possess. In his 'pittilesse' destruction of the Bower the Knight of Temperance violently represses what might reveal his own pre-existing vulnerability.

The violence of course is Spenser's invention, since he is author. And it reappears all too often in contexts where it is not explained by moral justice, namely in the handling of vulnerable heroines. Many of them undergo a symbolic loss of virginity by force. Amoret in the House of Busyrane has her heart taken out of her body, and she is chained to a brazen pillar. When Britomart releases her the pillar shakes and the wound heals over. Her entrapment was a graphic image of a woman being oppressively and tyrannically fucked. Even as a virgin again, she has this experience behind her. When Aemylia arranges to meet the squire who loves her, instead of him 'There was I found, contrary to my thought,/ Of this accursed Carle of hellish kind'. The Carl has a 'huge great nose' and 'two wide long eares' (4.7.18, 6). These details are phallic, he lives on 'ravin and on rape'. Going to meet her love object, Aemylia meets a phallic flesh-eater, who carries her off. Lastly Serena: her naked thighs are described as 'a triumphall Arch, and thereupon/ The spoiles of Princes hang'd, which were in battel won' (6.8.42). The spoils are an image for the pubic hair, but the simile associates the virginal vagina with something won by men in battle. Male conquest and force are always already present in the apparently virginal woman. Fighting Artegall Britomart is exposed to his 'lashing dreadfully at every part' (4.6.16). In her fight with Radigund, they

> spared not
> Their dainty parts, which nature had created
> So faire and tender, without staine or spot,
> For other uses, then they them translated;
> Which they now hackt and hewd, as if such use they hated
> (5.7.29)

What nature creates tender, the world demands to be hacked; what nature creates tender, the art *shows* to be hacked. Who really hates these parts? These are the parts which nearly seduce Guyon. Women who are virtuous give up or forcibly lose control over these dainty parts. The innocent use of dainty parts rarely happens in the poem. The much celebrated praise of virginity is, perhaps, praise of a fiction.

Where does this pattern of scarred virginities come from?

Woman first appears in Spenser's work as one who displaces a male partner to form a triangle of never-ending desire. Colin's desire for Rosalind is constructed as competition and denial of another. The anti-female texts relate, I think, to an always repressed desire for the male. At a time when sodomy was officially illegal if not taboo, we would expect this self-repression. Colin Clout associates what I take to be sodomy with his attack on corrupt courtiers, who profane the 'mightie mysteries' of love and make him serve 'for sordid uses'. Boys appear among the sex objects of the Bower of Bliss: naked boys depicted on a fountain and 'lascivious boyes' singing with women. Fancy in the House of Busyrane is a boy compared either to Ganymede

> Or that same daintie lad, which was so deare
> To great Alcides, that when as he dyde,
> He wailed womanlike with many a teare,
> And every wood, and every valley wyde
> He fild with Hylas name; the Nymphes eke Hylas cryde.

(3.12.7)

Both identifications are explicitly homoerotic. But the reference to 'great Alcides' (Hercules) seems not to denigrate the man's grief for his dead lover, even though it is 'womanlike'. The unevenness of tone alerts us to the problem. For Spenser sodomy was part of courtly corruption, but it also had a supposedly legitimate pastoral pedigree from Virgil's Eclogue 2 (a precedent wickedly exploited by Richard Barnefield (1595) for his own soft-porn homoerotic poems).

The homoeroticism emerges most plainly where there is apparently no need to be on guard against it. For example in the appearance of Tristram 'A goodly youth of amiable grace': it is explained that his good looks suggest he is 'borne of noble race' (6.2.5). The attention to the boy's looks is nominally justified, as it is again at stanza 24 in precisely the same way. He is neither pastoral lover nor corrupt courtier; his placeless 'wildness' may be taken to be innocent as is Belphoebe's (whom Tristram resembles with his buskins and boar-spear). Yet, as Tonkin (1972) notes, the stanzas describing Tristram are 'unnecessarily' elaborate for his role in the narrative. The feeling of homoeroticism is, however, mainly generated by the narrative structure. He tells how he intervened when a knight was mistreating a woman, and how that knight transferred his hostility against the woman to Tristram, 'me in lieu thereof revil'd againe' (11); and then how Tristram, like a serious Cupid, killed him with a dart. In the layers of the story, the woman is mistreated because her knight desired another woman whom he couldn't have; that second woman had been having sex with her own knight who is himself killed, while unarmed, by the first knight. So in killing the first knight Tristram, treated as a woman, avenges a knight who had been having sex. Desire and sex are at the heart of this story, where the innocent boy is involved in adult passions and is structurally placed alongside the desired woman (at two removes) and the love-making knight (at one remove). The structure creates a sexual involvement which the description remains innocent of: but 'his face so lovely sterne and coy' and 'his pregnant wit' are by now attributes of a sex object (24). The terms of his innocence are important: he has not 'spilt the blossome of my tender yeares/ In ydlesse' (31). There is moral approval of the discipline and work, but this is fused with a sexual approval. He has not 'spilt' himself in sensuality. Elsewhere this image can suggest, pejoratively, orgasm; spilling semen. The metaphor of spilling blossom is oddly mixed, because of its sexual function. Applied to women, the flower image denotes that which is to be picked, the virginity to be taken; 'flowers' was also a term for menstrual blood. The as-yet unspilt youth is blossoming—ready perhaps for the beholder to pluck. In economic terms he has not wasted time, but neither has he produced anything: he has been trained. Tristram is at the point of ending an eroticised apprenticeship; but has not entered the world of corrupting competition.

We are back where we began, with the desire for ideal masculinity. I introduced the idea as something related to Spenser's economic position. In re-stating it, I am stressing its sexual potency. The two aspects are not separable: Spenser was erotically engaged with enterprise. But the potentially explosive presence of that taboo sexuality, in a culture where the norm was dictated by the love-power language of the virgin queen, led to Spenser's restless and revealing engagement with desire and gender and his inability (or refusal) to reproduce the assumptions of so many of his contemporaries. The aim to reproduce dominant ideas may have made Spenser the arse-kissing poet; but the problem, for Marx as well as Spenser, is that arse-kissing has pleasures of its own.

# 3

# Art

## A. Poetry in *The Shepheardes Calender*

After a chapter looking at personal and sexual interrelations, we move to questions about individual identity. Spenser's thoughts about his art raised such questions, both about his role as poet and about human psyche in general. But once again class and economics relate intimately to the issue, since it was through his role as poet that Spenser sought to construct for himself standing in society. As before, we begin with analysis of a specific text: *The Shepheardes Calender*.

As a printed object, the text questions the dominance of poetry in that the woodcut illustrations and the editorial apparatus both contribute to the overall meaning. Furthermore, poetry seems to have no clear function as a medium of human communication: the first eclogue gives a sense that poetry can fully articulate Colin's inner emotion (by reflecting it in nature), but it is followed by an eclogue that questions the efficacy of poetic rhetoric, and then by a series of inconclusive debates. Though it is carefully dressed with all the apparatus belonging to a classical poet, and though it first appeared as an autonomous *book*, *The Shepheardes Calender* is a poem sceptical of the expressive potential of poetry.

Poetry is discussed most fully in the 'October' eclogue, in the person of Cuddie who feels his art is treated with scorn by audiences and patrons. The Argument says that poetry is 'no arte, but a divine gift and heavenly instinct not to bee gotten by laboure and learning, but adorned with both' (p. 456). The eclogue, however, speaks of poetry in economic relations. Every time Piers attempts to encourage Cuddie to write, Cuddie says there's nothing in it for him. Piers argues 'the prayse is better, then the price', but Cuddie asks 'who rewards him ere the more for thy?/ Or feedes him once the fuller by a graine?' (19, 33–34). Poetry is produced within specific social relations: 'I beate the bush, the byrds to them doe flye' (17): the image invokes the class divisions of aristocratic hunting sport. The theme is developed into a common Renaissance criticism, that the age has no heroes worth writing about, with which Piers, significantly, agrees. He adds that even the 'Princes pallace' has no place for poetry. Thus poetry is associated not with muses or divine instinct but with the economic relations of class and patronage.

The last section of the eclogue looks at the poet as private individual aspiring to spiritual heights through his own skill and emotion, particularly that of love. This Cuddie rejects: 'lordly love is such a Tyranne fell:/ That where he rules, all power he doth expell' (98–99). The language of politics is now used to describe the poet's inner life, and there's no solution. Only drunkenness produces poetry:

> if my temples were distaind with wine,
> And girt in girlonds of wild Yvie twine,
> How I could reare the Muse on stately stage,
>
> (110–12)

The classical image of poetic frenzy is here introduced as a sign of last resort for a poet alienated by lack of patronage and debilitated by personal relationships. The reference to the stage is not merely Cuddie's concern but, as we shall see, Spenser's. Poets who wrote for the stage worked within an artistic and social grouping which, by the late 1570s, looked as if it would bring economic rewards not wholly dependent on patronage. By contrast the alienated Cuddie would have to be drunk to write for the stage.

The image of the socially alienated poet tends to subvert contemporary ideas of the poet as legislator and educator. Many saw poetry, and especially rhetoric, as the means of creating obedience and civilised order, since they worked on audiences both to delight and persuade them. Successful poets aimed to have allegiances to, if not connections with, centres of political power. The aristocratic or genteel poet did not write for money, and indeed did not publish in our modern sense. But they did circulate their manuscripts among friends and associates, which is a form of publication; it's a form, however, which celebrates the elite, coterie nature of the readership that was privileged to be given a manuscript. By contrast, Cuddie is outside the centre of power, and his motives are explicitly economic. Cuddie will stop being a poet if he is unrewarded.

In 'October' the social role of poetry is firmly connected to the poet's inner life. Such an emphasis is characteristic of Spenser's thinking. The importance of the emphasis on inner life is political, because to accept that people have autonomous 'inner lives' is to suggest that they are, in some fundamental way, independent of the constraints of society or dominant culture, that they are 'free' individuals. Alongside this political importance we have to remember the (apparently contradictory) textual artifice; that's to say, when we find a poet 'speaking from his heart' in a text there is no reason to assume that this is a straightforward

93

expression of reality. The portrayal of an inner life and the sense of a person's private self are as much fictional constructions as the rest of the poetry. The stress on the poet as individual need not be a psychologically realistic portrait. But it is the fact of an 'inner life' which is important. Thus the poet can't be said automatically to speak as the voice of dominant culture. He (in Spenser's case) speaks as 'himself'. As an *individual* he can be alienated from dominant culture. This is not new with Spenser: in his Satires Thomas Wyatt adopts the speaking voice of one who is outside the centre of power. In the theory of the Italian Castelvetro, whose ideas were known to Spenser's well-travelled friend Philip Sidney, emphasis is laid on the value of (personal) experience in creating one's knowledge of the world. In Spenser's text a version of 'inner life' is created not only to criticise the state but also to question dominant ideas about the public function of poetry. The opposition of an inner life, with its language of 'personal' expression, to society, with its public rhetorics, may be described as critical humanism.

More examples may clarify: in the 'June' eclogue Colin is distressed about Rosalind and he resists Hobbinol's praise of his poetry: 'Nought weigh I, who my song doth prayse or blame, /Ne strive to winne renowne, or passe the rest' (73–74). The overall emphasis on the 'personal' melancholy of Colin becomes specifically focused here on a refusal of the ambition and competition produced by patronage systems. Colin adds: 'I wote my rymes bene rough, and rudely drest: / The fytter they, my carefull case to frame' (77–78). The rough style is supposedly appropriate and 'natural' to one who is melancholy and alienated. But clearly there is nothing really rough about the poetry here. It is a *pose* designed to express (though it really constructs) the anti-social melancholy, and as such it is a pose of refusal which relates politically to society. The tension between 'personal' and public is more pronounced, and more political, in

'September'. Hobbinol encourages Diggon to ease his melancholy by speaking about his grim experiences among corrupt 'Popish' shepherds (see Norbrook, 1984, on the religious position in the poem). Diggon's narrative is thus an 'expression' of his grief, a grief caused by religious and social corruption. A view of narrative, or poetry, as 'expression' gives authority to the individual who experiences and utters. The value given to the poet's experience means that he is no mere mouthpiece for received political truisms. This is marked here by the increasing embarrassment of Diggon's listener. Hobbinol's patient stoicism turns into criticism:

> Nowe Diggon, I see thou speakest to plaine:
> Better it were, a little to feyne,
> And cleanly cover, that cannot be cured.
> (136–38)

Diggon's style is too plain and (in a double-meaning) he speaks to (com) plain, so that his utterance in its intent and style challenges the status quo of society. Diggon claims that the church is still corrupt and that there's a need for constant vigilance. The dignity of Hobbinol's stoicism collapses: 'We bene of fleshe, men as other bee./ Why should we be bound to such miseree?' Instead of answering, Diggon returns to his personal problem: 'all this long tale,/ Nought easeth the care, that doth me forhaile./ What shall I doe?' (238–39, 242–44) And Hobbinol again offers sympathy. The shifts between public and private, the unanswered questions, all work to sharpen the critical humanism. Mere utterance cannot relieve Diggon; his emotion will be eased only by a change in the world. But Hobbinol cannot face this solution, and can offer comfort to Diggon only as a private distressed person. He cannot accept the links between 'inner life' and social structure, and thus he can never help Diggon. This is the contradiction in Hobbinol which is revealed by Diggon speaking 'to plaine'.

The tension between private and public surfaces again, so
critically, in the 'Aprill' eclogue where, as we have seen, the
hymn to Eliza coexists with the alienation of its maker and
singer. A pastoral narrative frames a formal iconic hymn to
royalty. There are two sorts of reality: the shepherds'
'natural' emotion and the external monarch, whose imagery
is reproduced by the self-consciously arty hymn. The word-
play on 'see' and 'seemely' precisely brings into tension
experience against rule-bound decorum. These tensions in
'Aprill', conscious or not, can perhaps be explained as
deriving from Spenser's sense of his own position as poet
within the social order. Some of *The Shepheardes Calender*
speaks the language of social and religious reform which
Spenser would have learnt from Langland and the medieval
tradition of 'prophecy'. This would have its appeal to the
more radical puritan gentry, who opposed royal policy
according to the dictates of their own religious consciences,
and perhaps to the circle around Leicester. But 'Aprill' also
works to display Spenser's skill in appropriate decorum, in
his knowledge of classics and pastoral tradition and in the
courtly hymn. Such display advertises his professional
qualifications as poet, and thus his employability by any
aristocrat and, potentially, the queen. Furthermore, his
artistry can construct a social position. In a society where
learning is a sign of social privilege, where knowledge is an
acquisition suitable to those who command (see Whigham,
1984), Spenser as 'learned author' can compete aesthetically
and artistically even where he is unprivileged economically.
He deliberately gave the appearance of a scholarly edition to
his first printed work in order to draw on the authoritative
status of classical poets, just as he showed in the 'Aprill'
eclogue that he could play Virgil to Elizabeth's Augustus.
Later, with *The Faerie Queene*, he was presenting to the
monarch a gift which could stand alongside those of
traditional aristocrats, irrespective of the social rank of the

giver. Literary ambition and the creation of a poet's role have their place within a fantasy of social advancement. Thus *The Shepheardes Calender* speaks from different poetic roles because it speaks from potentially different political alignments.

The very creation of a 'self' for the poet depended not on Spenser but on the power relations in the world in which he sought advancement. In Renaissance society a person's identity was defined by the social rank they held, by the property they owned, and by the sex they were born into: this last condition affected both social rank and the rights of property ownership. Spenser worked to create the 'rank' of professional poet who 'owned' his words. Thus the poet's image mirrors social structure. The stress on individual experience, the inner self, is likewise related to society in that it is a refusal to be anonymous alongside the other toadies. Spenser's versions of the 'self' are products both of his own economic and social interests and of the society which employed him. We ought therefore to look in more detail at the relations between self, language and patronage.

Language works on and persuades the individual, in a way that is very deep in that it gives individuals a sense of what they are as people, of their identity. We might ask whether we use language to express ourselves, or whether language gives us the illusion that we can use it to express ourselves. One of the most influential modern analyses of ideology shows how our sense of ourselves as individuals derives from the way in which we are addressed by ideology. We are told, for example, in the respective languages of various state institutions—in school, by laws, in family units—that we are freely choosing, free-thinking individuals. This concept is not born with us, but learnt (though we learn to think that it is born with us). The concept is also a myth since in capitalist society most of us are not free: the apparent freedom of some people depends on the exploitation and poverty of many others. Our concept of ourselves is constructed for us, by various activities and institutions of the state, and then learnt by us so thoroughly that we come to believe the concept is not learnt but natural, something we have always known. (Spenser's *View* has, let's recall, a similar stress on the importance of ideological 'framing'.) In studying a group of texts, say, those produced to represent Elizabeth I (in poems, speeches, pageants), we can see how those texts play a political role in defining the relations of monarch and society, in defining what a proper citizen is, etc. The texts are censored or allowed, sometimes even paid for, by those who have real power, both financial and military, to enforce their decisions. Such texts are useful because by spreading dominant ideas they make the naked (and expensive, and perhaps unpopular) display of force less necessary. This is the operation of an ideological apparatus, to which poets such as Spenser contribute.

The system of patronage was an economic structure producing artworks which coexisted with the printing and distribution of books on a commercial basis. It was a feudal formation in that authors linked themselves in bonds of personal loyalty to lords, and the economic relationship was spoken of in 'personal', even love, language. Authors were not primarily producers competing in an open market for custom. So that within a patronage system any intellectual activity is supposedly valued not for its own usefulness or entertainment, but for its ability to observe the conventions and procedures of feudal bonds: 'The glory, and grace, of a book written is muchwhat in the nobleness and magnificence of the patron' (Thomas Drant, 1567, quoted in Moore, 1982, p. 25). Intellectual activity is thus specifically affiliated to a dominant class, and performs the role of reproducing the ideas, the ideology, which help to maintain that class in dominance. Both Guicciardini (the Florentine historian, 1483–1540) and Thomas More (1478–1535) observe that the economic bond forces the writer to defer to, or adopt, the political outlook of the employer (see Gundersheimer in Lytle and Orgel, 1981). Patronage is therefore as much an ideological as an economic apparatus.

Spenser worked within a patronage system and derived his sense of himself from its ideological assumptions. As author, he writes from a position he has learnt; he takes up a position that ideology has made available to him (placed him in). But it's not that simple, since anybody's lived experiences are often in tension with their received ideas, and indeed with other ideologies. We know how critical Spenser was of a court which excluded him and how he gave himself a landed base. The alternative to patronage was to seek funding through the developing market and commercial distribution; many radical texts were produced by independent printers or autonomous theatre companies. In printing his works, thinking of them as books, Spenser refuses the anonymity of the patronage system and presents himself as autonomous writer, indeed as self-created laureate. Yet Spenser's views, which were obsessed with strong central authority, prevented him abandoning the patronage system: indeed he wanted a place for himself among the thought-police, as long as he was paid to say what he believed in. That's the problem.

Nevertheless, as readers, we can explore the ideological tensions in Spenser's work, over which he barely has control, and in doing so learn more about the relationship between artwork, social structure and ideology. This understanding is political. Political understanding can help change the world. (I doubt, however, that Spenser studies will: though you could encourage your local Cruise convoy—or its equivalent—into the ditch by hurling *The Faerie Queene* at it.)

## B. Patronising Persons

The pastoral figure of Colin Clout the poet appears again in *Colin Clout's Come Home Again* (1591) and in Book 6 of *The Faerie Queene* (1596). In the former he still speaks of his poetic 'roughness' but also claims that Cynthia (Elizabeth) 'joyd that country shepheard ought could fynd/ Worth harkening to, emongst the learned throng' (366–67): his 'rough' status gives him competitive supremacy precisely by appearing to be an outsider. But in *The Faerie Queene* it is less important that Colin is rustic than that he is privileged to play his pipe while the Graces dance. Thus Spenser's pastoral persona undergoes shifts in meaning.

The persona of Colin Clout had been previously used in Henry VIII's reign by the poet John Skelton as a mouthpiece for social and religious criticism. But even in his first, most explicitly reforming, published work, Spenser associates Colin with the 'love interest'. The persona is used more as an emotional individual, less as a critic. The role of poet-critic goes to Cuddie, of whom EK says: 'I doubte whether by Cuddie be specified the author selfe, or some other. For in the eyght Aeglogue the same person was brought in, singing a Cantion of Colins making, as he sayth. So that some doubt, that the persons be different' (p. 458). Both are, indeed, personas for Spenser, but he makes his closest identification with the non-critical melancholy Colin. In the revival of Colin some ten years later the persona was further amended.

Colin says he 'banisht had my selfe, like wight forlore,/ Into that waste, where I was quite forgot' (*Colin Clout* 182–83). His explanation of his exile presents it as his own sorrowful decision (though he implicitly blames those who forgot him). Later in the poem his exile is more articulately attributed to the corruptions of court, since he 'Durst not adventure such unknowen wayes,/ Nor trust the guile of fortunes blandishment' (670–71). This experience of corruption qualifies him to 'warne yong shepheards wandring wit' against the malicious competition of court, where each person seeks 'To thrust downe other into foule disgrace,/ Himselfe to raise' (684, 691–92). For this Colin, melancholic love-interest will not suffice to explain the alienation. He has a public role to perform. As defined in the whole poem, the role is bigger than social critic, for he is also told that as poet he is priest of the god of love and privileged to see the godhead. To see the poet as priest, and to give the 'simple' shepherd the power of divine expression, are clear invocations of the model—and the authority—of the classical definition of the poet.

Between *The Shepheardes Calender* and *Colin Clout* Spenser's social status shifted. He had been secretary, in quick succession, to the Bishop of Rochester, to the Earl of Leicester and to Lord Grey, and he had a job within the colonial administration. He had both worked in the centre of power and experienced its competitive rivalry. *The Shepheardes Calender* focuses on religious corruption; *Colin Clout* emphasises courtly behaviour and ambition—here the display of his professional suitability for the centre of power is combined with attacks on his detractors. Colin anticipates Cynthia's 'bounty most rewardful' but the effect of her patronage amounts to more than reward. His praise of her *gives him identity*:

> By wondring at thy Cynthiaes praise,
> Colin, thy selfe thou mak'st us more to wonder,
> And her upraising, doest thy selfe upraise.
> (353–55)

This statement, by another shepherd, interrupts Colin's musings:

> Why then do I base shepheard bold and blind,

> Presume the things so sacred to prophane?
> More fit it is t'adore with humble mind,
> The image of the heavens in shape humane.
>
> (348–51)

The dialogue form of the poem here allows Spenser to keep the pastoral Colin personally humble, while having other shepherds bequeath on him a new role (thus doing what real patrons should do). He displays both a respect for ideology (which he will not profane) and his own ideological skill, which can create wonder in others. This skill leads to an elevation of himself as an artist, which implies (but can never 'presume' to say) his social raising. Spenser can't leave this theme alone: Cuddie reproaches Colin for forgetting himself 'to mount so hie'. Colin replies that the effect of Cynthia's 'great excellence' is to lift him 'above the measure of my might': 'I feele my selfe like one yrapt in spright' (617, 620–22). Much hangs on what the poet's 'selfe' is—it is either the social place defined by birth and rank, or it is the emotional being which can be moved in spirit. The emotional being is more mobile, is not fixed in place by social structure. Its spiritual raptures imitate a social movement. Hence perhaps its interest to Spenser.

Colin explains that his authority for speaking in an elevated manner comes from the effect on him of the supreme patron, just as a priest is infused by the godhead. The language of emotion and spirit enables Spenser to elevate the status of Colin, and to give him authority to criticise the court, without speaking of money and social rank. In the latter of course Spenser himself had little authority. Colin's priestlike rapture expresses the royal influence on him. Thus it constructs a personal link between poet and absolute monarch. This link is useful in that it avoids analysis of a structure within which in reality Spenser had little power and where royal interests clashed with his own. The definition of 'selfe' in the poem relates closely to the ideology and structure of the patronage system, and in turn reproduces a particular version of the monarch's power.

The final appearance of Colin is in Faerie land (*Faerie Queene* 6.10), piping to the Graces and hence more privileged than the knight Calidore. It is a version of the status for which Spenser was continually striving. The poet who first appeared in the lowly pastoral persona regularly made claim to family links with aristocratic houses. In particular he traced connections with the Spencers of Althorp (indeed Princess Di may be related to him!). In his dedication of *The Teares of the Muses* to Lady Strange he tells her that 'the causes for which ye have thus deserved of me to be honoured (if honour it be at all) are, both your particular bounties, and also some private bands of affinitie, which it hath pleased your Ladiship to acknowledge'. The poem is devised 'both to intimate my humble affection to your Ladiship and also to make the same universallie knowen to the world; that by honouring you they might know me, and by knowing me they might honor you' (p. 480). Spenser candidly acknowledges the value to himself of making public a 'private' attachment. Rather than acting the lowly poet who abases himself while praising a great worthy, Spenser offers a reciprocal deal: his poetry will make her famous. To Lady Pembroke Spenser proffers his personal loyalty on the feudal model, while at the same time using the bond to repudiate his critics: 'sithens my late cumming into England, some frends of mine ... knowing with howe straight bandes of duetie I was tied to him [the late Sir Philip Sidney, Lady Pembroke's brother]: as also bound unto that noble house, ... have sought to revive them by upbraiding me' (p. 471). In the dedication of *Colin Clout* to Ralegh a similar anxiety is clear: he offers the 'simple pastorall' 'in part of paiment of the infinite debt in which I acknowledge my selfe bounden unto you, for your singular favours and sundrie good turnes shewed to me at my late being in England, and with your good countenance protect against the malice of evill mouthes, which are alwaies wide open to carpe at and misconstrue my simple meaning' (p. 536). The public display of 'private' favours between poet and great man gives the poet authority to answer his detractors. The dedication to Ralegh makes a careful distinction between the 'mean' style and the 'truth' of the matter. This distinction acts out the lowliness of poet-supplicant even while it asserts the authority of his 'truth'—an authority which the poetry consolidates. Similarly the dedicatory sonnets which prefaced the first part of *The Faerie Queene* were part of the usual humility puff, but were also sequentially arranged and tonally controlled to suggest the discrimination of the poet's own allegiances.

Spenser's Dedications are both assertive and insecure. He claimed family links with aristocrats (rather than merely offering his feudal service) in order to achieve an accepted place within the dominant order. But the system of patronage had as many difficulties as it had benefits. For poets such as Spenser it remained a primarily economic structure, despite the language of 'personal' loyalties and 'love'. His sceptical friend Gabriel Harvey pointed out the economic reality early on, in a letter published in 1580. Harvey says of Colin Clout that 'he peradventure, by the means of hir [Poetry's] special favour, and some personall priviledge, may happely live by *dying Pellicanes* [apparently an early poem of Spenser's], and purchase great landes, and Lordshippes, with the money, which his *Calendar* and *Dreames* have, and will affourde him' (p. 628). Harvey jokes about a real topic of interest. Spenser had already served Leicester, but it was not for a few years that he was to achieve the status of landed gentleman. The land was obtained through his salary and perks as an administrator in Ireland, rather than through his poetry (I disagree with those who say his verbal skill brought him status). The poetry's reward, a grant of £50 a year, came very late, and, although a sizeable sum, was peanuts compared with the wealth so obviously accrued by courtly entrepreneurs.

The patronage system is central to Spenser's poetic imagination. Most notoriously he interrupts his late marriage hymn *Prothalamion* to speak of his earlier patron:

> there standes a stately place,
> Where oft I gayned giftes and goodly grace
> Of that great Lord, which therein wont to dwell,
> Whose want too well now feeles my freendles case:
>
> (136–40)

Then he moves on to celebrate the rising star of the Earl of Essex. The image of his 'freendles case' recalls the persona who opens the poem, whose

> discontent of my long fruitlesse stay
> In Princes Court, and expectation vayne
> Of idle hopes, which still doe fly away,
> Like empty shaddowes, did aflict my brayne,
>
> (6–9)

Within the celebration of the marriage, with all its verbal trickery and ornate imagery, is another narrative based on the discontented persona of the creator. While the connection between aristocrats and wealthy gentry is imagined as a mythic pageant, the poet's own connection with aristocrats is a mixture of frank disappointment and extravagant, but necessary, optimism. It is only in the narrative of the poet that economic relations are stated baldly.

The effort to explain and relate to the patronage system produces texts which, for us, make beautifully clear the contradictions around the poet's role in this type of economic order. As with his political outlook, it is Spenser's own peculiar position which leads to this unique clarity. Let's look at a 'lesser known' poem.

In *The Teares of the Muses* each Muse tells why she weeps. Clio describes the plight of historians and scholars:

> learned Impes that wont to shoote up still,
> And grow to hight of kingdomes government
> They underkeep, and with their spredding armes
> Doo beat their buds, that perish through their harmes.
>
> (75–78)

The peers who should sustain 'true wisedome' deem it 'a base thing' to be learned, and 'In th'eyes of people they put all their praise, / And onely boast of Armes and Auncestrie' (93–94). The critique here envisages a world in which social movement can happen ('learned Impes' can shoot up) though it happens only for the few who are worthy. It praises learning and 'vertuous deeds' as ideal values which continue, recorded by scholarship, even where the supreme authority of peers decays in its obligations. Like Spenser's, Clio's vision makes room for the ascending scholar and for the scholar's absolute importance as guardian of eternal virtue. It also sees that the scholar's place depends on the power of peers, and, simultaneously, that peers are inclined not to reward. The attack on peers comes from one who needs their favour, and who recognises only them as the dominant power in society. Their failure to reward is presented as a moral failing. This presentation obscures what in reality is a problem deriving from the peers' place in social structure. The moral idea is attractive because moral failings can be more easily remedied than can structures of society.

The text is at pains to stress the individual specialness of the scholar. Thalia condemns the vulgarisation of theatres,

> Rolling in rymes of shameles ribaudrie

Without regard, or due Decorum kept,
Each idle wit at will presumes to make,
And doth the Learneds taske upon him take.
                                    (213–16)

Vulgar upstart writers try to please the masses, just as peers seek praise in 'th'eyes of people'. It is typical of Spenser's outlook that he will condemn both 'shameles ribaudrie' *and* boasting of 'Armes and Auncestrie'. Opposed to the vulgar writers is the memory of the dead author, Willy, who scorned the 'boldnes of such base-borne men' and chose 'to sit in idle Cell,/ Than so himselfe to mockerie to sell' (219, 221–22). The thematic engagement with the quality of, and market for, writing produces an apparent contradiction in the text. Earlier the blame was focused on those who kept down 'learned Impes'; here the poetry performs the function of keeping down the new theatre writers. The give-away word is 'base-borne': it is not precisely the artistic skill of the dramatists which is troubling, but their improper ascent from low birth. The contradiction derives from Spenser's own ambition and seeks appropriate reward for his own art, and needs to devalue the art of those working—successfully—to the same end: the theatre was the most rapidly expanding artform in Spenser's lifetime. While Spenser looks for reward to a grouping he partly distrusts, the peers, he condemns the rewards which come from a mass market, from which his personal circumstances cut him off. The realities of status and market pressurise the text into both commending *and* attacking the ascent of 'learned Impes'.

The 'independence' of the proper scholar is again articulated by Urania, who says that although she is despised

I feede on sweet contentment of my thought,
And please my selfe with mine owne selfe-delight,

> In contemplation of things heavenlie wrought.
> (524–26)

The notion, and valuing, of an independent self is, as we've seen before, part of the ideological product of the apparatus of patronage. It is not, however, necessarily the intended product, for the apparatus itself works to insist on the bonds of loyalty between writer and patron and the self-definition of the writer only through the approval of the patron. Spenser's own insistence on his individuality comes because for him the patronage system does not fully work, and because he is aware of its economic limits. While he gained lands through 'non-aristocratic' means, as a writer he still offers himself for employment by aristocratic patrons. The dual placing of Spenser in both the colonial apparatus and the patronage apparatus produced contradictions in his self-identity which would not perhaps appear in a poet of gentry origins.

Spenser saves for last in *Teares* his tribute to Poetry. In making it he shows a knowledge of the ideological function of the patronage system. In the past 'none might professe/ But Princes and high Priests that secret skill,/ The sacred lawes therein they wont expresse' (559–61). Now, however,

> nor Prince nor Priest doth her maintayne,
> But suffer her prophaned for to bee
> Of the base vulgar, that with hands uncleane
> Dares to pollute her hidden mysterie.
> (564–67)

Poetry loses its 'mysterie' when handled by the vulgar, a point of more importance, suggests Spenser, to princes than to poets. For poetry was once a special language of rulers and created their mystique (the play on 'secret'/'sacred' is important). Here is Spenser linking himself with the

ART

dominant class by showing a proper respect for, and ability in, their mystery of poetry. Furthermore, his anxiety to have poetry patronised leads him to spell out how poetry maintains the mystique of power against attempts at democratisation. The language about 'mystery' and 'sacred laws' is ideological, and the ideology functions to maintain a division of power. Spenser is not so fully implicated in the system that he merely begs for patronage: he knows that he offers a political tool.

Calliope warns what happens if learning is not encouraged:

Ne doo they care to have the auncestrie
Of th' old Heroes memorizde anew,
Ne doo they care that late posteritie
Should know their names, or speak their praises dew:
But die forgot from whence at first they sprong,
As they themselves shalbe forgot ere long.

(439–44)

The nobility has degenerated both in its 'desire of worthie deeds' and its scorn for learning. Deeds alone are not enough, because the cultural re-telling of past deeds has its effect in the present. Poetry can construct respect for the current ruling elite by remembering their glorious forebears (and it can use the same technique to criticise). Within the political function of this ideological apparatus, the poet is as important to the nobleman as is his family: 'What bootes it then to come from glorious/ Forefathers, or to have been nobly bredd?', and what is the distinction between good and bad 'If none of neither mention should make/ Nor out of dust their memories awake?' (445–46, 449–50). The poet is necessary to keep 'awake' the great family's authority, which is seen to depend on its heroism more than its inherited wealth. In this way the poet, and the poet's ideological constructions, serve the dominant order. Furthermore, 'if good were not praised more than ill,/ None would choose goodnes of his owne freewill' (455-56). The urgency of Spenser's attempt to show the social importance of poetry leads him to admit the dominant order is—or is potentially—corrupt. There'd be no point in having morally legislative poetry if people were by nature inclined to good.

And here is the deep contradiction. In offering his art as a necessary means for maintaining a dominant order, the poet is seeking employment from an order he concedes is corrupt. The poet can speak of ideal virtue but there is no guarantee that those to whom he speaks will value the message. Calliope says that

> noble Peeres whom I was wont to raise
> Now onely seeke for pleasure, nought for praise.
>
> Their great revenues all in sumptuous pride
> They spend, that nought to learning they may spare;
> And the rich fee which Poets wont divide,
> Now Parasites and Sycophants doo share:
>
> (467-72)

Despite all the scholarly independence and the claimed value of poetry, the poet is powerless to control the peer's money. In choosing to depend on the patronage system, this poet has chosen to keep in power an order over which he has no economic control. I suspect it was the knowledge of this contradiction which produced Spenser's frequent ragings against the public theatres, where writers worked with players to get cash from a paying audience, largely independent of patronage. Those writers borrowed chunks of Spenser's writing for their plays, and not always, like Marlowe, in mockery. But it was a form of work Spenser could not undertake. Quite apart from his being in Ireland, Spenser had a contempt for and fear of a mass audience (which was possibly fed by his experience in Ireland). The contempt was part of his pride in his specialist scholarship and his respect for the idea (if not the practice) of great families. These two ideals in their turn functioned to show his separateness from that mass out of which he himself so painstakingly rose.

A number of similar ideas are present in *The Ruines of Time*, which I shall use to reiterate a couple of points. The text of *The Ruines* is spoken by a personification of the ancient city of Verlame and it's a tribute to the dead members of the Sidney family, in particular Sir Philip. Verlame criticises poets for not mourning Sir Philip and includes in their number Colin Clout, who will not 'tell his sorrow to the listning rout/ Of shepherd groomes' (227–28). There are two images of poets here. Most poets move with the times and don't praise a dead hero, and Spenser includes himself as Colin with these (although he makes his private emotion something special). The other, and major, poetic authority belongs instead to Verlame, who instructs the poets 'with my mourning plaints your plaint increase' (238). This authority derives from her superior, because more extensive and more authentic, emotion. The expression of appropriate grief for the Sidneys will produce the necessary poem. Here is the supreme poet as truly emotional individual. Spenser as Verlame, not as Colin, produces the needed elegy. So there is both a valuing of the independent poetic emotion and a knowledge of the constraints on poets in a real world of patronage.

Poetry is said to withstand mutability and thus to repay aristocratic investment. Verlame says that to ascend to heaven 'with vertuous deeds' you must 'with sweete Poets verse be glorifide' (426–27). But then there are those like him who first was raised 'for vertuous parts' who now in his age 'Lets none shoot up, that nigh him planted bee' (451, 453). The power of the great does not necessarily follow the

111

dictates of learning or morality. Such a view of the value and denigration of poetry is sceptical because it suggests there's no automatic link between good deeds and recognition, between virtue and social significance. Publicly perceived virtue has to be invented. The powerful man may be good only insofar as he is praised as good. Yet his immediate power is not affected by the way he is praised.

After such scepticism Verlame retires into an eloquent personal grief:

> who so els that sits in highest seate
> Of this worlds glorie, worshipped of all,
> Ne feareth change of time, nor fortunes threate,
> Let him behold the horror of my fall,
>
> (463–66)

Verlame's grief indicts a supreme earthly ruler; Spenser at second hand, perhaps, voices his own alienation and neglect. The very sincerity of the emotion makes the speaker of significance, even to the mightiest ruler. The poet Spenser, authorised by his poet's 'selfe', may speak to and at the queen. The apparent social power of Verlame's emotion and moral example is a construction made possible by the poetic medium. In reality that personal emotion has no power: it is eloquent only within the context of the poem. On the other hand, whether the poem is eloquent in the context of society is as much up to the patron as the poet. The poem is offered as an elegy for a great family, but it also expresses the poet's distress (speaking through Verlame). The personal emotion is both an answer to, and a product of, the patronage system.

When, at the end of *Ruines*, the narrator sees 'tragicke Pageants' for Sidney, they confirm his own sense of alienation. I want to use this response in order to move on to talk more generally about artworks and audiences.

Spenser is frequently conscious of a need to explain why

his art was not always patronised. The problem is frequently with patrons and audience rather than the art. Spenser is careful to note that in places owned by evil people, such as the House of Pride and the Bower of Bliss, there is still good workmanship. In particular the problem is with responses to art. In *Teares* he observed that peers sometimes looked for pleasure rather than praise; in *Ruines* Verlame warns against undiscriminating audiences who 'when the courting masker louteth lowe,/ Him true in heart and trustie do you trow' (202–3). Throughout *The Faerie Queene* Spenser makes contemptuous references to theatres and masques.

I have suggested briefly why Spenser may have disliked the public professional theatres. But another explanation has to account for his dislike of masques, which were an artform most closely associated with the elite entertainments of royal or aristocratic houses. The explanation takes us into Spenser's views about audience response to artwork, which we have to see now not merely as the economic relationship of patronage but as a theory of psychology. I shall try to clarify this from *The Faerie Queene*.

Guyon going to the Bower of Bliss arrives in a harbour shaped 'like an halfe Theatre' and is greeted by performances as he journeys. In the Bower everything

> that may dayntiest fantasie aggrate,
> Was poured forth with plentifull dispence,
> And made there to abound with lavish affluence.
> (2.12.42)

In Spenser's terms the affluence spent on fantasy is misspent. At the entrance is a porter called Genius 'That secretly doth us procure to fall,/ Through guilefull semblaunts, which he makes us see' (48). There is a horror of being encouraged to see falsely and believing the vision. Guyon violently refuses the porter's courtesy and breaks his magic staff. Once inside,

113

Guyon wonders at the beauty of the place

> yet suffred no delight
> To sincke into his sence, nor mind affect,
> But passed forth, and lookt still forward right,
> Bridling his will, and maistering his might:
>
> (53)

Delight is imagined to operate as a poison that invades the being: the resistance and rebelliousness of the Irish had been attributed to long years of 'sensual *immunity*' (Canny, 1976, p.128; my emphasis). The implication here is that individuals can control whether they feel delight, and thus resist disease. Where the control comes from is uncertain, however, for both Guyon's will and his might have to be bridled and mastered. Presumably reason does the controlling, but the text does not say so. Furthermore, we have to remember a point that emerged from the analysis of the wrestling maidens in this episode: even while he may repel the external incursions of delight, there are *already inside* the personality of the knight elements which he needs—and indeed fails—to control. The Palmer has to prevent Guyon's eyes from wandering, because he already has in him the capacity to embrace pleasure, however illicit.

While Guyon smashes the staff of Genius and shatters the cup of Excess, he is drawn to the maidens. Yet the maidens, who are deliberately wanton, might appear a more obvious threat than Excess, who seems so apparently hospitable. The important contrast lies in what each offers. Excess openly offers the cup, greeting all strangers in a 'goodly' way. The maidens, as we know, arrange their clothes both to expose and conceal. Guyon's desire is produced by denial rather than generosity. This is in keeping with his role as questor who overcomes obstacles. Significantly it is easy to reject the '*idle* curtesie' of Genius. Something freely offered is not, in these terms, as exciting as possession that has to be fought for. The pleasure that almost traps Guyon is not only already in him, it is shaped by his very role in life.

His response to temptations is to destroy them. The episode educates the reader into the need for iconoclasm (see Greenblatt, 1980, on this episode). The violence is deliberately shocking: 'taking it out of her tender hond/ The cup to ground did violently cast'(57): 'tender' sets up expectations that are thwarted. At the end Guyon counsels the misled Verdant and then breaks down the Bower and its 'Pallace brave': 'Ne ought their goodly workmanship might save/ Them from the tempest of his wrathfulnesse'(83). The power of the individual questor is, through the act of iconoclasm, reasserted over the pleasurable and tempting artworks. Yet at the same time, as so many commentators have noted, the poetic descriptions have elicited in readers a sense of beauty. The imagery describing the wrestling maidens is very carefully worked, and their moral status in the narrative doesn't destroy the imaginative pleasure fostered by the text. The episode engages and delights the reader with what is to be destroyed. Spenser takes the trouble to compare the Bower with Parnassus and Eden, among other mythic beauty-spots, in order to exploit the fact that these places are famous not just for beauty but for moral good, such as poetic creation and divine creation. Part of Spenser's project is his familiar one, of educating readers through their own shifting responses to the text. And partly he is defining his own role as the poet who destroys Parnassus. The workmanship destroyed by Guyon is on one level Acrasia's, and on another it is Spenser's own ornate creativity. Spenser the hard-headed adventurer narrates the necessary smashing of Spenserian fantasy poetry.

But we may be able to make a further explanation of the iconoclasm. Let's return to Genius, here seen as the opposite to the good Genius who is 'our Selfe' and 'oft of secret ills bids us beware'(47) (the 'our' here is presumably again denoting 'us, the male readers'). The Bower's Genius is instead 'foe of life' who makes us see 'guilefull semblaunts'. Both Geniuses make us see things which either help us (as males) or lead to our fall. Spenser links them by giving them the same name. Furthermore, he provides no explanation of how 'we' are to tell which Genius is working upon us with his visions at any one time. The evil Genius is comely and almost unnaturally good-looking; his garment is unsuited to 'manly exercize'. He is the reverse of the masculine hero and Guyon forcefully rejects him (breaking the phallic staff). But he is said to represent something that is always and already part of ourself. If we recall the chapter on sex, we could say that the violence which is so necessary for Guyon to define his own identity and role is also necessary for Spenser: so he can insist on a particular version of himself, as poet—and as sexual being.

The most famous definition of responses to the artwork, and of the poet's role, came very late in Spenser's writing life: the episode when Calidore interrupts Colin's piping to the Graces. The vision of the Graces disappears when Calidore enters, and Colin 'for fell despight/ Of that displeasure, broke his bag-pipe quight' (6.10.18). Calidore destroys what he attempts to join. His pleasure is both voyeuristic and never-satisfied. And the courtly knight can't replace what he has ended: 'being gone, none can them bring in place,/ But whom they of themselves list so to grace'(20). Thus it is up to Colin alone to describe and explain the vision, the poet producing the text for the knight.

Only the poet has the satisfaction of both watching and contributing to the dance of the Graces. The knight can spy on it and hear about it, but cannot be present. He can also destroy the poet's bliss. The simple poet knows the true skills of civility taught by the Graces: his courtly knowledge is derived from an experience which he as poet is privileged to have. The Knight of Courtesy practises a set of rules, which frequently cause social disruption, and in the story of Coridon and Pastorella amount to man-management, bribery and deception (in *A View* Spenser speaks of forcibly instating 'civil conversation' as a mode of suppressing subject peoples). The episode is not a clash of civility and savagery but a delineation of the limits of poetry and courtesy. Courtesy is the violent intrusion, and the Knight of Courtesy is always doomed to be unfulfilled in that he cannot for himself recall the vision. He deprives Colin of his 'loves deare sight' and causes the poet's alienation. This is a cynical account of the place of poetry in supposedly civilised society, but it is part of the attack on courtliness in the whole Book. Readers of the episode, themselves literate and hence privileged, are carefully placed. The narrative offers them both the vision of the Graces and knowledge of the presence of the secret viewer, Calidore 'Beholding all, yet of them unespyde'(11). For the reader there is never the simple pleasure of Colin's oneness with the Graces; the illicit other is always present, the vision always tempered by voyeurism.

To conclude this episode and mark Colin's disappearance from the poem, there is a compliment to Gloriana: Colin apologises to her for taking the time to praise his own beloved. The poem here had come very close to presenting Colin's pleasure in love as complete, without any mention of the supreme patron and ruler who is supposedly loved by all. The abrupt introduction (or 'memory') of Elizabeth has an effect on the narrative continuity similar to that of Calidore on Colin's piping. The break is an indication of Spenser's knowledge of the real power relations. The need to praise Elizabeth eventuallly surfaces, and in doing so it undermines the security of the image of the blessed, blissful and originally self-contained poet.

The episode of Colin and Calidore discusses the creation of and response to artworks, and inevitably it defines the poet's role. Here at the end of his life, and as a successful poet, Spenser is still connecting alienation with the role of poet. We might see his constant return to Colin as a need produced from his own insecurity with dominant society. In seeing himself as Colin, Spenser gives to the poet-figure a society, a role, an audience; all of these are partly familiar from an already existing mode of writing, the pastoral, and are hence secure and coherent. Colin is an image of himself over which Spenser has control, and thus provides in fiction a solution to the problems of a confused real world. In *Colin Clout* the poet is asked why he left the happy place where he could gain wealth in order to return to 'this barrein soyle'. Colin speaks of the 'enormities' and 'unknowen wayes' at court (655–70), and prefers the 'utmost hardnesse' of his sheep. He has continuity in his life as shepherd which makes it preferable, despite its toughness, to the uncertainty of court life. His place of origin and job of work can be set in opposition to the scramble for wealth at court. By contrast, the real Spenser did not succeed in remaining employed at the centre of power (if he ever wanted it); as a colonial administrator his position was always threatened by the native population; as a landed gentleman he had to fight law cases over his lands and had trouble making ends meet; the poetry he created to make himself the laureate of a generation was vulnerable both to the government censor and to the flames of the Irish rebels. The image of Colin gives simplicity and purpose to what was always a problem. And in turn the image liberates Spenser: it allows him to speak of the contradictions at the centre of power. Despite the presence of the queen there are '*continually*' enormities at court. When Spenser claims to be directly writing about Elizabeth he cannot say this, for she is seen as an ideal. The fantasy figure of Colin is necessary to him because it embodies an alternative to—and a resolution of—the otherwise intolerable reality of a permanently flawed rule.

I have recalled an analysis made in a previous chapter in order to lead into the concluding point. When I stress the difficulties of Spenser's life, I am conscious that he achieved a fame in his lifetime which has been consolidated by critical writing in modern times. But the fame does not preclude a position I see as basically unstable within Elizabethan society. It is that instability which produces, through Spenser's engagement with his own problems and difficulties, a revealing analysis of that society. We have seen some of the difficulties about both money and sexuality. In writing about poetry and patronage Spenser ends up telling us very much more than other poets about why the Renaissance persona had to be created, why the insistance on 'truth' is necessary, how poetry relates to ideology, how culture relates to economics. In a sense it's an old story: distressed conservatives produce fascinatingly radical analyses that they themselves can't tolerate.

# Chronology

1552–4   Born probably in London (the family originating, probably, in Lancashire).

1561   Enters Merchant Taylors' School as a 'poor scholar'.

1569   Anonymously publishes epigrams and sonnets (which are translations, of Marot 'Visions by Petrarch', and 'Visions of Bellay') in Jan van der Noodt's fiercely anti-Catholic compilation *A Theatre wherein be represented as wel the miseries and calamities that follow the voluptuous Worldlings.*
20 May, admitted to Pembroke Hall, Cambridge as a sizar (a poor scholar who had to perform servant's tasks).

1570   Friendship with Gabriel Harvey, Fellow of Pembroke, begins.

1573   Graduates BA.

1576   Awarded MA. Some conjecture that he visited the north, possibly Lancashire, in these years.

1577   Conjectured to be in Ireland (based on reference in *A View of . . . Ireland* to the execution of Murrogh

O'Brien in July this year).

1578      Secretary to John Young, Bishop of Rochester. In December is apparently with Harvey in London (being described by Harvey as a dandy).

1579      In service of Earl of Leicester. In October he writes to Harvey claiming to be on familiar terms with Edward Dyer and Philip Sidney.

27 October, marriage of an 'Edmounde Spenser' to Maccabaeus Chylde at St Margaret's, Westminster. They had two children: Katherine and Sylvanus.

5 December, *The Shepheardes Calender* entered in Stationers' Register (Prefatory Epistle dated 10 April 1579). There is reference to a number of 'lost' works.

1580      Publication of correspondence with Harvey; in addition to reference to more 'lost' works— including *Nine Comoedies*, there is mention of *The Faerie Queene*.

12 August, probably arrives with Arthur Lord Grey de Wilton, to whom he is now private secretary, in Ireland, where Grey is the new Lord Deputy. In November he is present at the massacre at Smerwick, organised by Grey.

1581      In March takes up a seven-year appointment as a registrar attached to the Irish Court of Chancery. Second edition of *The Shepheardes Calender*.

6 December, leases, and quickly forfeits, Abbey and Manor of Enniscorthy, Co. Wexford; leases New Ross, Co. Wexford.

1582      Leases a house in Dublin; also New Abbey, Kilcullen (Co. Kildare); attains rank of landed gentleman.

1583      Two-year appointment as commissioner for musters, Co. Kildare.

1584      Deputy to the Clerk of the Council of Munster,

|       | Lodowick Bryskett. |
|-------|--------------------|
| 1585  | Prebendary of Effin, attached to Limerick Cathedral. |
| 1586  | Third edition of *The Shepheardes Calender*. Sonnet to Harvey, dated 18 July, Dublin. Assigned the ruined castle of Kilcolman, Co. Cork, with its estate of 3000 acres (forfeited by the rebel Earl of Desmond). |
| 1588  | Reference (by Abraham Fraunce) to Book 2 of *The Faerie Queene*; the poem was probably circulating in manuscript in London. |
| 1589  | Ralegh visits Ireland, and stays on an estate near Kilcolman. In October travels with Ralegh to England, and has an audience with Elizabeth I. |
|       | 1 December, *The Faerie Queene* entered in Stationers' Register. This year begin the legal battles with Lord Roche over estates. |
| 1590  | Books 1–3 of *The Faerie Queene* published. |
|       | 26 October, granted possession 'for ever, in fee farm' of Kilcolman; establishes colony of six English families. |
| 1591  | Publication of *Complaints: Containing sundrie small Poemes of the Worlds Vanitie* (comprising nine poems); *Daphnaida*; fourth edition of *The Shepheardes Calender*. Part of *Complaints* was suppressed, perhaps because of the satire in *Mother Hubberds Tale*, taken to be directed at Lord Burghley. |
|       | 25 February, granted life pension of £50 a year by Elizabeth I. Returns to clerical duties in Ireland. |
| 1594  | Queen's Justice for Co. Cork. |
|       | 11 June, marries Elizabeth Boyle, who is related to Sir Richard Boyle, who became first Earl of Cork; one child: Peregrine. |
| 1595  | *Amoretti* and *Epithalamion* published; *Colin Clouts Come Home Again*, dated 27 December, 1591, Kilcolman, published (volume also includes *Astrophel* and other elegies on death of Sidney). |

1596    Books 4–6 of *The Faerie Queene* published, with second edition of Books 1–3; *Fowre Hymnes* published; *Prothalamion* published.

1597    Fifth edition of *The Shepheardes Calender*. Purchase of the castle of Renny, Co. Cork, and Buttevant Abbey.

1598    Sheriff designate of Cork. In October the castle of Kilcolman is sacked and burned by Irish rebels; the family flee to Cork.
        14 April, *A viewe of the present state of Ireland* entered in Stationers' Register (but only published in 1633).
        9 December, travels to London with messages for the Privy Council from the governor of Munster.

1599    13 January, dies in Westminster and buried in Westminster Abbey. The royal instruction to erect a memorial was not carried out.

1609    Folio edition of *The Faerie Queene*, books 1–6 (includes 'Cantos of Mutabilitie').

1620    Memorial erected in Westminster Abbey.

# Bibliography

## Reading For Each Chapter

### Texts of Spenser

All books and articles referred to in the text are listed either in the section 'Reading for each Chapter' or in the list of 'Works Consulted'. The reason for the two separate lists is to highlight, and introduce the reader to, the most useful material, in a form more accessible than the conventional bibliographical list.

I have used the *Poetical Works*, ed. J. C. Smith and E. de Selincourt (Oxford, 1912/1970) and *Spenser's Prose Works*, ed. R. Gottfried (Baltimore, 1949) (I have modernised spelling and punctuation in my quotations from *A View*). The notes are useful in *The Works of Edmund Spenser – A Variorum Edition*, ed. E. Greenlaw *et al.* (Baltimore, 1932–49), 10 vols; also *The Faerie Queene*, ed. A. C. Hamilton (London, 1977).

**Introduction**
On the New Historicism, begin with Louis Adrian Montrose 'Renaissance Literary Studies and the Subject of History' and Jean Howard 'The New Historicism in Renaissance Studies', both in *English Literary Renaissance* 16 (1986), 5, 13; and also Jonathan Dollimore's Introduction to *Political Shakespeare*, ed. Dollimore and A. Sinfield (Manchester, 1985). New Historicism has its origins in Marxism and the discipline of cultural materialism, but it is currently an academic bandwagon onto which many non- or anti-Marxists are jumping. For Marxist and cultural materialist accounts go straight to Robert Weimann, *Structure and Society in Literary History* (Baltimore, 1984) and Raymond Williams, 'Base and Superstructure in Marxist Cultural Theory' in *Problems in Materialism and Culture* (London, 1980). The 'hidden agenda' of much New Historicism is to eradicate the importance of class and economic structure as forces in cultural formation, and to replace them with other explanatory theories based on psychoanalysis, post-structuralism or the work of the 'historian of ideas' Michel Foucault (who is used even by such a brilliant scholar as Montrose). See Stephen Greenblatt, Introduction to *Renaissance Self-Fashioning* (psychoanalytic/'anthropological'); Jonathan Goldberg, 'The Politics of Renaissance Literature' *ELH* 49 (1982), 514 (anti-Marxist); Michael McCanles, 'The Authentic Discourse of the Renaissance' *Diacritics* 10 (1980), 77 (post-structuralist).

**Chapter 1**
The most concise analysis of feudalism and absolutism in England is Perry Anderson, *Lineages of the Absolutist State* (London, 1974). Other useful works are: Goran Therborn, *What Does the Ruling Class Do When It Rules?*

(London, 1978) [sections on feudalism]; Rodney Hilton (ed.), *The Transition from Feudalism to Capitalism* (London, 1976); David Cressy, 'Describing the Social Order of Elizabethan and Stuart England' *Literature and History* 3 (1976). Also the opening paragraphs of Richard Halpern, 'John Skelton and the Poetics of Primitive Accumulation' in *Literary Theory/Renaissance Texts*, ed. P. Parker and D. Quint (Baltimore, 1986).

On Ireland at this period, I have used Nicholas Canny, *The Elizabethan Conquest of Ireland* (Hassocks, 1976). Also see Philip Edwards, *Threshold of a Nation* (Cambridge, 1979) and the Commentary in W. L. Renwick (ed.), *A View of the Present State of Ireland* (Oxford, 1970). For the intellectual and political context of the ideas in *A View*, see Nicholas Canny, 'Edmund Spenser and the Development of an Anglo-Irish Identity' *The Yearbook of English Studies* 13 (1983), 1.

For Spenser in Ireland, and his life in general, the classic work is still A. C. Judson, *The Life of Edmund Spenser* (Baltimore, 1945). The most informative books on Spenser's historical and religious context are David Norbrook, *Poetry and Politics in the English Renaissance* (London, 1984); Anthea Hume, *Edmund Spenser: Protestant Poet* (Cambridge, 1984); Michael O'Connell, *Mirror and Veil* (Chapel Hill, 1977). For a stimulating overview of religion and literature, see Alan Sinfield, *Literature in Protestant England* (London, 1982).

An exciting book that makes use of Spenser's Irish experience is Stephen Greenblatt, *Renaissance Self-Fashioning* (Chicago, 1980). A scholar doing the best work on Spenser, and the Renaissance in general, is Louis Adrian Montrose. All his essays should be read, even if you read nothing else. They appear throughout these notes. For brilliant introductions to pastoral, see 'Of Gentlemen and Shepherds: The Politics of Elizabethan

Pastoral Form' *ELH* 50 (1983) (this builds on Raymond Williams, *The Country and the City* (London, 1973); '"Eliza, Queene of shepheardes", and the Pastoral of Power' *ELR* 10 (1980); '"The perfecte paterne of a Poete": The Poetics of Courtship in *The Shepheardes Calender*' *Texas Studies in Language and Literature* 21 (1979), 34; 'Interpreting Spenser's February Eclogue' *Spenser Studies* 2 (1981), 67. Also on pastoral, and qualifying Montrose, Annabel Patterson, 'Re-opening the Green Cabinet: Clement Marot and Edmund Spenser' *English Literary Renaissance* 16 (1986), 44.

The main theoretical text underlying my method here and elsewhere is Pierre Macherey, *A Theory of Literary Production*, tr. G. Wall (London, 1978); his method is explained clearly by Catherine Belsey, *Critical Practice* (London, 1980) and by Tony Bennett, *Formalism and Marxism* (London, 1979). The method is used simply by Brean Hammond, *Pope* (Brighton, 1986). For more of Macherey, see his essay with Etienne Balibar, 'Literature as an Ideological Form' *Oxford Literary Review* 3 (1978), 4.

**Chapter 2**

In this chapter I have used Frederic Jameson, *The Political Unconscious* (London, 1983); see also his essay 'The Ideology of the Text' *Salmagundi* 31/2 (1975/6), 204. Useful books on ideology are: Goran Therborn, *The Ideology of Power and the Power of Ideology* (London, 1980) and Jorge Larrain, *The Concept of Ideology* (London, 1979).

Steadily more work is being done on women in this period, not all of it good and some pretty reactionary. Some of the best work is the earliest: Sheila Rowbotham, *Hidden from History* (London, 1974). See also Linda Woodbridge, *Women and the English Renaissance* (Brighton, 1983);

Lawrence Stone, *The Family, Sex and Marriage in England 1500–1800* (London, 1977); Keith Wrightson, *English Society 1580–1680* (London, 1982). For ideas about fertility, pregnancy and gender see Angus McLaren, *Reproductive Rituals* (London, 1984) and Brian Easlea, *Science and Sexual Oppression* (London, 1981).

For love language and the politics of courtship, see Arthur Marotti, '"Love is not love": Elizabethan Sonnet Sequences and the Social Order' *ELH* 49 (1982), 396; Louis Adrian Montrose, 'Celebration and Insinuation: Sir Philip Sidney and the Motives of Elizabethan Courtship' *Renaissance Drama* n.s.8 (1977), 3.

On Elizabeth I, see Alison Heisch, 'Queen Elizabeth and the Persistence of Patriarchy' *Feminist Review* 4 (1980), 45; Louis Adrian Montrose, 'The Elizabethan Subject and the Spenserian Text' in *Literary Theory/Renaissance Texts* (*op. cit.*); '"Shaping Fantasies": Figurations of Gender and Power in Elizabethan Culture' *Representations* 1 (1983); 'Gifts and Reasons: The Contexts of Peele's *Araygnment of Paris*' *ELH* 47 (1980), 433; Frances Yates, *Astraea: The Imperial Theme in the Sixteenth Century* (London, 1975); Roy Strong, *The Cult of Elizabeth* (London, 1977). For general remarks about fighting women and Renaissance gender discussion, see Simon Shepherd, *Amazons and Warrior Women* (Brighton, 1981). Maureen Quilligan, *Milton's Spenser* (Ithaca and London, 1983) assumes *FQ* is written to Elizabeth, and must be read as a work directed to a female reader (see also Dallett in Works Consulted).

On the sexual and male gaze, see E. Ann Kaplan, 'Is the Gaze Male' in *Desire*, ed. A. Snitow *et al.* (London, 1984); Laura Mulvey, 'Visual Pleasure and Narrative Cinema' *Screen* 16 (1975), 6. For paintings, John Berger, *Ways of Seeing* (London, 1972). On Ovidianism and voyeurism, Leonard Barkan, 'Diana and Actaeon: The Myth as Synthesis' *ELR* 10 (1980); on Petrarch and the gaze,

Nancy Vickers, 'Diana Described: Scattered Woman and Scattered Rhyme' *Critical Inquiry* 8 (1981). Also perhaps C. S. Lewis, *The Allegory of Love* (Oxford, 1936).

For homosexuality in this period, see Alan Bray, *Homosexuality in Renaissance England* (London, 1982): also Simon Shepherd, *Marlowe and the Politics of Elizabethan Theatre* (Brighton, 1986).

**Chapter 3**

Some useful accounts of rhetoric and language theory in the Renaissance are: Terence Hawkes, *Shakespeare's Talking Animals* (London, 1973); Frank Whigham, *Ambition and Privilege* (Berkeley, 1984); Hugh Kearney, *Scholars and Gentlemen* (London, 1970); R. F. Jones, *The Triumph of the English Language* (Oxford, 1953); Walter Ong, *Ramus, Method and the Decay of Dialogue* (Cambridge, Mass., 1958).

In this chapter, I have drawn on Louis Althusser's essay 'Ideological State Apparatuses' in *Lenin and Philosophy* (London and New York, 1971); see also Therborn's *The Power of Ideology* (*op. cit.*). For the context of Althusser, see Perry Anderson, *Considerations on Western Marxism* (London, 1976).

On patronage, see *Patronage in the Renaissance*, ed. Guy Fitch Lytle and Stephen Orgel (Princeton, 1981). For Spenser and the Earl of Leicester, see Eleanor Rosenberg, *Leicester Patron of Letters* (New York, 1955). Very useful is Wallace McCaffery, 'Place and Patronage in Elizabethan Politics' in *Elizabethan Government and Society*, ed. S. T. Bindoff (London, 1961).

On the role of the poet, particularly Spenser's, see Richard Helgerson, *Self-Crowned Laureates* (Berkeley, 1983) (though I disagree both with his categories and the formalist/moralistic form of analysis); Richard Mallette, 'Spenser's Portrait of the Artist in *The Shepheardes*

*Calender* and *Colin Clouts Come Home Againe*' SEL 19 (1979), 19 (vitiated by a bourgeois sentimentalism); D. L. Miller, 'Authorship, Anonymity and *The Shepheardes Calender*' *Modern Language Quarterly* 40 (1979) and 'Spenser's Vocation, Spenser's Career' *ELH* 50 (1983) (the latter assimilates the sort of work done by Montrose to a metaphysical/transhistorical position).

Work on the development of ideas of individuality is often not easy to read. Greenblatt's *Renaissance Self-Fashioning* (*op. cit.*) is very accessible; see also his 'Psychoanalysis and Renaissance Culture' and Montrose 'The Elizabethan Subject and the Spenserian Text' in *Literary Theory/Renaissance Texts, op. cit.*; William Kerrigan, 'Articulation of the Ego in the Renaissance' in *Psychiatry and the Humanities*, ed. J. H. Smith (Yale, 1980); Thomas Greene, 'The Flexibility of the Self in Renaissance Literature' in *The Disciplines of Criticism*, ed. P. Demetz et al. (New Haven, 1968).

## Works Consulted

This is not a complete list: I have tended to mention more modern works and I have dropped the most useless—though not all of *these* are useful.

### Abbreviations

*ELH*: A Journal of English Literary History; *ELR*: English Literary Renaissance; *MLQ*: Modern Language Quarterly; *PMLA*: Publications of the Modern Language Association of America; *SEL*: Studies in English Literature.

Alpers, P. J. *The Poetry of The Faerie Queene* (Princeton, 1967).

Anderson, D. ' "Unto My Selfe Alone": Spenser's Plenary Epithalamium' *Spenser Studies* 5 (1985).

Barnefield, R. *Poems* (1595), ed. E. Arber (London, 1896).

Bean, J. C. 'Making the Daimonic Personal' *MLQ* 40 (1979).

Berger, H. *The Allegorical Temper* (New Haven, 1957).

Berger, H. 'Orpheus, Pan, and the Poetics of Misogyny' *ELH* 50 (1983).

Bernard, J. D. 'Spenser's Pastoral and the *Amoretti*' *ELH* 47 (1980).

Bernheimer, R. *Wild Men in the Middle Ages* (New York, 1970).

Bond, R. B. 'Supplantation in the Elizabethan Court: The Theme of Spenser's February Eclogue' *Spenser Studies* 2 (1981).

Brinkley, R. A. 'Spenser's *Muiopotmos* and the Politics of Metamorphosis' *ELH* 48 (1981).

Cain, T. H. *Praise in The Faerie Queene* (Lincoln, USA, 1978).

Cheney, D. *Spenser's Image of Nature* (New Haven, 1966).

Coles *Notes on The Faerie Queene*, H. M. Priest (London, 1968).

Cummings, R. M. (ed.) *Spenser – The Critical Heritage* (London, 1971).

Dallett, J. B. 'Ideas of Sight in *The Faerie Queene*' *ELH* 27 (1960).

Davies, Stevie, *The Idea of Woman in Renaissance Literature* (Brighton, 1986).

Dunseath, T. K. *Spenser's Allegory of Justice in The Faerie Queene V* (Princeton, 1968).

Elliott, J. R. (ed.) *The Prince of Poets* (New York, 1968) [for essays on Colin Clout, the Cave of Mammon].

Evans, M. *Spenser's Anatomy of Heroism* (Cambridge, 1970).

Fletcher, A. *The Prophetic Moment* (Chicago/London, 1971).

Frushell, R. C. and Vondersmith, B. J. *Contemporary Thought on Edmund Spenser* (Carbondale and London, 1975).

Greene, T. M. 'Spenser and the Epithalamic Convention' in

Elliott, J. R. (1968).

Grennan, E. 'Language and Politics: A Note on Some Metaphors in Spenser's A *View of Ireland*' *Spenser Studies* 3 (1982).

Hankins, J. E. *Source and Meaning in Spenser's Allegory* (Oxford, 1971).

Hoffman, N. J. *Spenser's Pastorals* (Baltimore, 1977).

Johnson, L. S. 'Elizabeth, Bride and Queen: A Study of Spenser's April Eclogue and the Metaphors of English Protestantism' *Spenser Studies* 2 (1981).

McCanles, M. '*The Shepheardes Calender* as Document and Monument' *SEL* 22 (1982).

Montrose, L. A. 'A Poetics of Renaissance Culture' *Criticism* 23 (1981).

Moore, D. *The Politics of Spenser's Complaints and Sidney's Philisides Poems* (Salzburg, 1982).

Okerlund, A. N. 'Spenser's Wanton Maidens: Reader Psychology and the Bower of Bliss' *PMLA* 88 (1973).

Sessions, W. A. 'Spenser's Georgics' *ELR* 10 (1980).

Skura, M. A. *The Literary Use of the Psychoanalytic Process* (New Haven, 1981), chapter 4.

Starkey, D. 'Representation Through Intimacy' in *Symbols and Sentiments*, ed. I. Lewis (London, 1977).

Stone, L. *The Crisis of the Aristocracy 1558-1641* (Oxford, 1965).

Tonkin, H. *Spenser's Courteous Pastoral* (Oxford, 1972).

Tonkin, H. 'Spenser's Garden of Adonis and Britomart's Quest' *PMLA* 88 (1973).

Watson, E. A. F. *Spenser* (London, 1967).

Wells, R. H. *Spenser's Faerie Queene and the Cult of Elizabeth* (London, 1983).

Wynne-Davies, M. *Arthurian Poetry in the English Renaissance* (unpublished PhD thesis, University of London, 1985).

Yeats, W. B. 'Edmund Spenser' (1902) in *Essays and Introductions* (London 1961).

# Index

133